RESTORING
DIGNITY
NOURISHING
HOPE

RESTORING DIGNITY NOURISHING HOPE

Developing Mutuality in Mission

Edited by
Jonathan Barnes and
Peter E. Makari

THE PILGRIM PRESS
CLEVELAND

The Pilgrim Press, 700 Prospect Avenue, Cleveland, Ohio 44115
thepilgrimpress.com
© 2016 by Jonathan Barnes and Peter E. Makari

Scripture quotations, unless otherwise noted, are from the New Revised Standard Version of the Bible, © 1989 by the Division of Christian Education of the National Council of the Churches of Christ in the United States of America, and are used by permission. Changes have been made for inclusivity.

Printed in the United States of America on acid-free paper

19   18   17   16   4   3   2   1

ISBN 978-0-8298-2037-9

contents

FOREWORD · VII
Julia Brown Karimu and James Moos

INTRODUCTION: Mission in the Twenty-first Century · IX
Carlos F. Cardoza-Orlandi

PART I: THE CURRENT CONTEXT OF MISSION

1   PARTNERSHIP: Pitfalls and Possibilities · 1
Prince Dibeela, Majaha Nhliziyo, and Jonathan Barnes

2   MISSION IN A GLOBALIZED WORLD · 11
Beverly Eileen Mitchell

PART II: NURTURING COMMUNITY

3   RECEIVING IN PARTNERSHIP: Opening Our Hearts · 23
*Gloria Vicente Canú, Phyllis Byrd, and Susan McNeely
edited by Catherine Nichols*

4   RELATIONSHIPS: Why and How We Serve in Mission · 35
*Elena Huegel, Judy Chan, and Jeffrey Mensendiek
edited by Catherine Nichols*

PART III: SHARING THE STORY

5 MISSION AND INTERRELIGIOUS DIALOGUE
The Case of Christians and Muslims in the Middle East · 49
Mohammad Sammak

6 EVANGELISM: Reconciling with God, Reconciling with Others · 59
*Balázs Ódor, Shin Seung-Min, and Elida Quevedo
edited by Derek Duncan*

PART IV: WORKING FOR PEACE WITH JUSTICE

7 CHANGED THROUGH SERVING: Engaging in Advocacy · 75
Peter Shober, Scott Nicholson, and Grace Bunker

8 HOW CAN ADVOCACY HEAL? · 87
Mery Kolimon and Karen Campbell-Nelson

PART V: DEVELOPING RESOURCES

9 MARY, MARTHA, AND MONEY · 101
Tom Morse

10 LEARNING FROM OUR GLOBAL PARTNERS · 113
Linda McCrae

NOTES · 123

RECOMMENDED READING · 129

CONTRIBUTORS · 137

| 59 | 9780829820379 | 59 |

WH: Aisle 11 Row: Bay 3
Bay: Shelf 5

ZBM.8DHQ

Title:	Restoring Dignity, Nourishing Hope: Developing Mutuality in Mission
Cond:	Very Good
User:	bc_ravneetk
Station:	Lister-03
Date:	2025-03-03 15:04:08 (UTC)
Account:	Zoom Books Company
Orig Loc:	Aisle 11 Bay 3 Shelf 5
mSKU:	ZBM.8DHQ
vSKU:	ZBV.082982037X.VG
Seq#:	59
unit_id:	27119968
width:	0.39 in
rank:	6,726,281

ZBV.082982037X.VG

delist unit# 27119968

xxxxx

foreword

Global Ministries is a unique ecumenical partnership for mission of the Christian Church (Disciples of Christ) and the United Church of Christ. Both North American denominations share a deep commitment to the unity of the church, a long history of cooperation and a common understanding of God's call to mission.

Every generation must respond anew to God's call to mission by participating in God's work of love and justice in the world. Looking back at more than two centuries of mission history by Global Ministries and its component bodies, there is much to be learned, much to be thankful for, and much that should not be repeated. It is easy to stereotype the mission activity of earlier generations in one of two directions—as being entirely colonial and paternalistic on the one hand, or consistently noble and heroic on the other. The reality is that mission is carried out by human beings who are, at one and the same time, both frail and faithful.

There are instances in our mission history in which the church and its missionaries colluded with colonial powers and acted in paternalistic ways, the result being that human dignity was damaged and suffering was inflicted. Some missionaries who were sent to serve among Native Americans, for example, forced native children to attend distant boarding schools. The disregard for family structures and cultural norms left deep wounds that are still in need of healing.

On the other hand, missionaries also established educational and health care institutions throughout the world, many of which continue

VII

to operate to the benefit of all—Christians as well as people of other faiths and traditions. Many also showed unconditional and self-sacrificial love, as did those from our heritage who chose to stay in Nanjing, China, during the massacre of 1937–38. An estimated three hundred thousand people were killed in the massacre, but many were also saved by missionaries who risked their own lives to create safety zones in which tens of thousands of Chinese took refuge. Today, those missionaries are memorialized in the Nanjing Massacre Museum.

In Global Ministries, we seek to respond prayerfully and faithfully to God's call to mission in our own day. We believe this calling can best be discerned in conversation with our partners around the world who understand their ministries and contexts far better than we do. In this way, we can avoid some of the pitfalls of the past while building upon successes. At the same time, working in mutuality opens us up to receiving the rich gifts and graces that global partners have to share with us. In other words, in God's mission all give and all receive.

Restoring Dignity, Nourishing Hope: Developing Mutuality in Mission was written to share some best practices and perspectives on mission with local churches. Its chapters are written by lay people, theologians, missionaries, and global partners. They are organized according to the Global Ministries' Strategic Plan, which outlines four strategic directions: Nurturing Community with domestic and overseas partners, Working for Peace with Justice by mobilizing God's people for advocacy, Sharing the Story of God's mission, and Developing Resources for mission. Each chapter includes discussion questions to assist with further reflection.

Mission is not an optional activity for the church, but is central to its existence. As the theologian Emile Brunner once wrote, "The church exists by mission as fire exists by burning."[1] It is our prayer that *Restoring Dignity, Nourishing Hope: Developing Mutuality in Mission* will enable those fires to burn more brightly.

Rev. Julia Brown Karimu and Rev. Dr. James Moos, co-executives
Global Ministries

i n t r o d u c t i o n

Mission in the Twenty-first Century
Carlos F. Cardoza-Orlandi

It is always exciting to have a fresh reading of the practices and theologies of Christian mission! I emphasize practices and theologies because in my vocational world the predominant inclination is the theological—the reflective, critical perspective. In the field of mission studies, there is a growing attention to the relationship between practices and theologies. In fact, the practices of Christian mission without the critical theological reflection and the critical theological reflection without the practices render Christian mission irrelevant and frequently harmful to the communities involved in Christian mission.

For example, in my almost thirty years of teaching mission studies in academic, congregational, and grassroots settings, students always raise the following question: "Christian missionaries had good intentions when engaging in Christian mission. Why can't we focus on the missionaries' good intentions rather than on identifying and discussing the problems they created and their role in the colonial system—all of that negative history?" Early in my vocation as a theological educator, my answer was straightforward, "Because the road to hell is paved with good intentions." As my vocational grounding matured, it was evident that my answer was as limited as my students' assumptions about missionary practices, theologies, and good intentions. There are no perfect missionary practices and there are no perfect mission theologies! So, what do we have left? We

x | INTRODUCTION

have the imperative to support missional practices and the challenge to nourish missional theologies that best embody the Christian communities' gospel story. Hence, both missional practices and missional theologies are sources for fostering a living faith deeply grounded in the daily life experience of our contexts and communities. Mission practices and theologies are intrinsic to the life of the Christian church.

When struggling with the debate between theology and practices, I always remind myself what bell hooks, one of my vocational mentors, taught me in her book *Teaching to Transgress*. She states:

> When our lived experience of theorizing [theologizing] is fundamentally linked to processes of self-discovery, of collective liberation, no gap exists between theory [mission theologies] and practice [practices of mission]. Indeed, what such experience makes more evident is the bond between the two—that ultimately reciprocal process wherein one enables the other.[1]

Now, mission practices and theologies should not be prescription-made programs or template-type missionary structures that can be "applied" to any Christian community. The best examples of mission theologies and practices are those developed and deeply grounded in their context, seeking the meaning of the gospel in all creation, and with an in-depth discernment and imagination of what God is doing in the world in order to co-participate in God's creation. Christian communities that aim to have healthy mission theologies and practices should expect their Christian identity to be fluid and open to the direction and challenge of the Holy Spirit.

For example, I was always surprised by the powerful words of a Lord's Prayer I saw in an addiction rehabilitation center on the Mexican side of the Mexico-Arizona border. This commentary on the Lord's Prayer demands a critical evaluation of the relationship between worship, particularly the prayer and Lord's Supper, and our personal and collective mission. Every Sunday, as I recite the Lord's Prayer in the Eucharistic celebration, I am reminded of it.

Do not call me "Father" if every day you do not behave as my child;

Do not say, "Our," if you live isolated in your selfishness;

Do not say, "Who art in Heaven," if you only think about earthly/ material things;

Do not say, "hallowed be thy name," if you invoke it with your lips, but your heart is far from [God];

Do not say, "thy Kingdom come," if you mistake it for your material success;

Do not say, "thy will be done," if you do not accept the will when it is painful;

Do not say, "give us this day our daily bread," if you do not worry about the hungry;

Do not say, "forgive us our debts/trespasses," if you bear your brother and sister a grudge;

Do not say, "lead us not into temptation," if you do not avoid occasions to sin;

Do not say, "deliver us from evil," if you do not fight evil;

Do not say, "Amen," if you have not taken seriously the words of the Lord's Prayer.[2]

This devotional and missional resource is a challenge to my Christian identity—a summons never to allow my Christian identity to become draconian, unyielding, obtuse, but rather responsive, flexible, sharp.

This should also be our experience as part of the body of Christ, the church in the world. As Christian communities, we seek new meanings and embodiments of the gospel. Our collective Christian identity is nourished by new experiences—some requiring time for reflection and discernment and others immediately giving insight and direction to our lives—that provide new bearings and stimulus to be faithful co-participants in God's missionary work in creation.

This collection of essays offers the reader different ways of integrating missional practices and theologies. The essays address current missional

XII | INTRODUCTION

issues, juxtaposing testimonies and practical implications with thoughtful critical analysis and educational guidelines. The reader can intuitively discover the integration and mutual enrichment between missional practices and theologies. These essays also provide a window through which to view the diversity of missional Christian identities and practices in the world, even going beyond Christian perspectives. Yet, within this diversity of Christian identities the reader will also discover multiple common practices and theologies. Our ecumenical grounding will be challenged, yet it will also be nourished and guided in a different direction.

These reflections also provide an understanding of Christian mission from a global perspective. Hence, the reader discovers Christian mission as it is embodied in different regions of the world and a fresh calling to ground Christian mission in our local, contextual communities. As a theological educator, I see in these essays a source for missional formation. Students and participants in missional work will find that the testimonies, the theological recommendations and suggestions, and the stories connected to the gospel stories from different parts of the world are mirrors of what Christian communities can do and learn when engaged in God's missionary work in the world and in one's immediate context. Moreover, these essays remind the reader that Christian mission comes from the marginalized. The vitality in missional theologies and practices comes from people at the margins and pushes for Christians to rediscover the gospel and its missional character by dwelling and living in solidarity with Christians in mission in the margins.

Finally, the Christian religion is undergoing a demographic shift. Most of the Christians of the world—and the regions where Christianity is growing—are in Africa, Asia, and Latin America. These reflections give witness to the vitality of the faith in these regions and to the cross-cultural life that the Christians from these regions offer our Christian communities in the United States and Canada. Yet, in many of our denominational and congregational circles, our sisters and brothers from the Global South (a term commonly used to refer to countries in Africa, Latin and South

America, and parts of Asia) continue to be an appendix in our church scenarios. In many Christian communities—whether growing, stagnant, or declining—we continue to have a "missional weekend" highlighting our trips and measuring up to the "missional" expectation of our time—cross-cultural missional tourism with no connection between our experiences in the Global South and the challenges in our immediate communities.

These essays are a gift from Global Ministries. They are an opportunity for our Christian communities to rediscover the passion of God for God's creation, the vitality of the Christian gospel in the life of people all around the world, but particularly in those who are marginalized—including our own people in the United States and Canada—and the formula that keeps the church alive: Christian mission is a never-ending journey of being pleasantly surprised and challenged by the Holy Spirit to live the gospel anew!

I | THE CURRENT CONTEXT OF MISSION

1

PARTNERSHIP
Pitfalls and Possibilities

Prince Dibeela, Majaha Nhliziyo, and Jonathan Barnes

PARTNERSHIP: WHAT DO WE MEAN?

Partnership. It is the term that many churches, including the Christian Church (Disciples of Christ) and the United Church of Christ, use to describe international relationships. If you go through the training that Global Ministries provides for missionaries, much of what is discussed deals with issues of partnership. Global Ministries stresses that our relationships with partners should be marked by solidarity, mutuality (where all involved both give and receive), and community. When thinking about mission, it is tempting to say, "This is it! This is the way that mission should be practiced!"

The truth, however, is that we live in a complex and uneven world. Engaging in international partnerships in a world divided in so many ways, yet a world also intimately connected through global economic systems and communication networks, is no easy task. For North Americans to practice partnership in ways that actually foster relationships of solidarity, mutuality, and community, it is helpful to have a basic understanding of how the term has been used in the past, the importance of our

2 | THE CURRENT CONTEXT OF MISSION

perceptions in these relationships, and some possible practices that can be gleaned from experience.

Living in an uneven world is not new. Most of Protestant mission history took place in an era when Western countries were expanding their economic, cultural, and military reach through the acquisition of colonial territories. Historians speak of mission's collusion with colonial governments in regards to the "three Cs"—Christianity, commerce, and "civilization"—and not necessarily in that order. It is important to note that there are examples of missionaries who sought to live in more equitable relationships with indigenous peoples. It is also true that for many of those who served, as well as those who sent them, the building of schools, hospitals, and efforts in Bible translation came from a place of care and concern. Even today, many partners continue to express gratitude for the presence and witness of missionaries from the beginning of Protestant mission history in the nineteenth century, affirming the role the mission boards played in their establishment and history, as well as during exceedingly difficult episodes in history such as the Armenian Genocide and the Nanjing Massacre.

However, despite these examples, the mood of the times made these early efforts at partnership extremely difficult. A story about a conversation between Henry Venn, secretary of the Church Missionary Society in the mid-1800s, and an African merchant from Sierra Leone captures the struggle between equality and paternalism. As the merchant discussed his many travels, Venn asked him, "Now, if you can afford to spend money on travelling for your pleasure, why don't you contribute something to the support of your own clergy, instead of leaving it all to us in England?" The merchant replied, "Mr. Venn, treat us like men, and we will behave like men; but so long as you treat us like children, we shall behave like children. Let us manage our own Church affairs, and we shall pay our own clergy."[1] Throughout Protestant mission history, the tension between the desire for genuine relationships of friendship and care over against a paternalism that sees Western culture and norms as superior has continued to make international partnerships difficult.

The term "partnership" has a long history of usage in mission engagement. It was first mentioned at a large mission gathering in Edinburgh, Scotland, in 1910. In a later world mission conference at Jerusalem in 1928, the term gained even more currency in describing the relationships between those who sent and received missionaries. At about the same time, however, partnership became the official policy of the British government in relation to their colonies. The British could see that one day in the future their colonies would become independent, so they used partnership to signal a relationship more advanced than that of trusteeship while still maintaining some power over these territories and peoples. Given this history, it is not surprising that the term was used in mission practice in much the same way as was intended by the British and, while sounding like a term of equality and mutuality, actually signaled a relationship of paternalism and dependence. It was only during the time of decolonization, which began following World War II, that the demands of churches in the Global South for a different quality of relationship began to be heard by churches in North America and Europe.

While the situation today is markedly different than during the era in which this history took place, when one looks at discussions about partnership over the past few decades, it is clear that living in mutuality with partners continues to be difficult. In 1980, a report on ecumenical relations noted that "many churches, especially those of the United States, 'still have not abandoned the image of missionary activity as one-way traffic. From us to them. From developed to underdeveloped countries.'"[2] A report from the Bangalore Consultation, a World Council of Churches sponsored event in 1996 that focused on the practice of partnership, said that "one of the most serious impediments to realizing partnership is the 'traditional and ever-present understanding of mission that we find to be based on a nineteenth-century missionary agenda of building outposts of sending churches, agencies, and organizations.'"[3] More recently, at the Athens meeting of the Commission on World Mission and Evangelism in 2005, it was stated that in international church relationships, "paternalism keeps

4 | THE CURRENT CONTEXT OF MISSION

being a practice. A paternalism . . . working with an agenda which lacks self-criticism . . . while enjoying to evaluate the life and problems of 'those others down there.'"[4] Despite the fact that many churches and missionaries have, over the past few decades, been seeking to live out partnerships of solidarity and fellowship, mission can still be viewed as what "we" in the Western world do "to" or "for" others.

Today, especially within churches associated with the ecumenical movement, partnership is a key concept in our mission relationships. From the local to the national church setting, we desire to have relationships with others, and partnership generally serves as the key lens through which these relationships are understood. Problems can occur, however, when we use the term uncritically, ignoring the lessons of history and assuming that we all are using it in the same way to mean the same quality of relationships. When this is the case, we can very easily reproduce paternalistic relationships, even though our desire is the opposite.

If one only looks at this history, it is easy to want to throw our hands up in the air in despair. We still live in a world of disparities—unequal access to financial resources, adequate education and healthcare, and basic human needs such as water, food, and shelter. If partnership has been so problematic in the past, how can we hope to experience life-giving relationships in which there is true mutuality today—receiving and sharing on all sides?

In order to better understand a possible way forward, the writers of this chapter share the ways in which perceptions of the world and history shape the way we practice partnership, as well as offer some guidelines or "best practices" for partnership engagement, seeking to deal honestly with issues of power and paternalism.

PERCEPTIONS OF PARTNERSHIP

Mission is not an option for any local church. In Emile Brunner's famous words, "The church exists by mission, just as fire exists by burning."[5] In some churches, we must cultivate an "outwardness," a "sent-ness," in the mindset of Christians. Every church should be outward looking. Partnership begins when we receive the stranger into our church, when we lift others up in our prayers of petition, and when we structure the call of our ministries such that it is not just about "us." Partnership should be integral to the life of the local church as well as of the individual Christian. It is not something to be expressed only "out there" in international relationships, but it also relates to local cross-cultural relationships "at home."

But many of us are already outward looking. We care deeply for others and feel called to make a difference in the world. However, we experience problems in our mission relationships when we engage or reach out without first understanding our own assumptions and preconceptions towards those with whom we engage. Do we understand mission as something we do "to" or "for" others, or do we engage "with" others? As churches participating in mission, efforts to understand this history, as well as the preconceived (mis)perceptions we have inherited, should be taken seriously in seeking to correct the paternalistic approaches of past centuries. Recognizing past errors can lead to a commitment to work out new models of mission engagement. New models will help minimize the negative impact of the complex and uneven world in which mission occurs. Therefore, education in mission programs must play a key role in sharpening perceptions of ourselves and those with whom we work.

The history, geography, and language of mission must be the subject of in-depth focus in the church's curriculum. Many of the old notions about mission need to be reviewed and exposed because they are inappropriate for this time in history. Chief among these worldviews is the mentality of mission as moving from the "developed" to the "underdeveloped," from the dominant center of North America and Europe to a weak and impoverished periphery of the Global South.

As we look into the history of mission engagement, we should also point out exceptional cases of good practice. Among the examples of such good practice is the relatively unknown John Philip of the London Missionary Society, who served in South Africa in the early to mid-1800s. John

6 | THE CURRENT CONTEXT OF MISSION

Philip vehemently opposed the enslavement of the African people as practiced by the colonialists, hunters/poachers, traders, and settlers and was someone who stood prophetically against the dominant powers of his time.

When it comes to language, do we need to reconsider words like "missionary," as they may carry too much baggage from the past? Terms like "mission co-worker" would be closer to the thinking behind new perceptions of mission. While the term "partnership" has been misused in the past as a cover for paternalistic relationships, at its best it refers to a "relationship based on trust, mutual recognition and reciprocal interchange."[6]

Another lesson is that mission should be multidirectional, from everywhere to everywhere, in a network of transcultural and intracultural movements of people committed to a spirit of mutual service. Jesus in Acts 1:8 states, "But you will receive power when the Holy Spirit has come upon you; and you will be my witnesses in Jerusalem, in all Judea and Samaria, and to the ends of the earth." This passage illustrates the kind of understanding of mission characterized by solidarity or comradeship, mutuality or friendship, and community or *Ubuntu* (an African concept meaning "I am because we are," emphasizing the importance of human relationships). In this story, the disciples are told to stay in Jerusalem until they have received power. Once this power is received, they shall be "witnesses" from Jerusalem, in Judea and Samaria, and to the ends of the earth.

While the linear movement of the mission plan in this story is contestable, its beauty for our discussion lies in the mention of the promise of power. Is this an admission of the reality of power dynamics in mission? Power exists in all relationships. However, it is the type or content of power that should be questioned. Power dynamics in mission should be acknowledged as a sociological reality and dealt with openly. In so doing, we can avoid the errors of the past when mission work was often carried out under the "three Cs" of Christianity, commerce, and "civilization." One cannot imagine that the disciples were completely passive while just waiting for the promise of power. Could it be an overstatement to suggest that they were engaged in an educational and training exercise? Surely they could not have just gone out without any knowledge of the geography, history, and cultures of the people they were going to meet on the way! In addition, what about the support systems from Jerusalem as the "initial base" and from farther afield from among the people receiving them? Our contention is that receiving power was not limited to an intensely individual religious experience, but was a more comprehensive exercise among the whole body of believers, those who were sent and those who accepted them and their message.

A third important lesson is that the kind of mission education that helps us critically consider the types of relationships we have impacts not only Christians in North America, but the entire church around the world. For instance, there are misplaced expectations and distortions of what it means to be a missionary that are popularized by television or in books. These distortions affect not only the views of mission in North America, but they have also been internalized by many in the Global South. Sometimes there is only one story being told, so we believe it is the entire truth and not just a partial and incomplete view. Let all of us tell our stories, because in so doing we open up our worldviews and create opportunities for better understanding through dialogue. For instance, family or church school quiz games like "Where in the world is . . . (Kinshasa/Soweto/Accra/Seattle/Indianapolis)" could be created. And we should not only learn about the names of places around the world, but also study the peoples, cultures, and traditions of these places. Such games could be adapted to promote Global Ministries's core values of presence, mutuality, community, justice and peace. Both the READY youth curriculum and the REACH adult curriculum, available on the Global Ministries website (globalministries.org), are two resources that individuals and churches can use to think deeply about our calling to mission engagement and how we live that out.

There could also be deliberate efforts to share, enjoy, and celebrate the mutuality of spiritual, liturgical, and cultural riches, especially from those who have been pushed to the margins. This would help re-instill the value of human dignity that has been stolen from many in the Global South—peoples portrayed as passive and needing outside direction and resources by the paternalistic systems of empire. Steve Biko, whose death is remembered every year in South Africa on September 12, once said that "the most potent weapon of the oppressor is the mind of the oppressed."[7]

We therefore consider mission education and practices that lead to "decolonizing the mind" as teaching the essence of true partnership. An open-minded approach frees us to debate and allow for the inflow of God's Spirit. This would test the maturity of our leadership to discern how to move forward together. As D. Preman Niles notes in his book *From East to West—Rethinking Christian Mission* (a must read for a discussion on mission!),

> We never begin anything; we never end anything.
> We begin where someone else left off;
> And we end where someone begins.
> And across all our lives are written the words "Move on"![8]

POSSIBILITIES FOR THE FUTURE

If mutuality, both giving and receiving, is to be meaningful, it does not do any good to transform the mission thinking in the North but not in the South. We need centers of mission training in the partner churches, which will offer the same kind of transformed mission thinking. Otherwise, mission partners coming to the South would be disillusioned because the mentality would still be "what can you do for us?" instead of how we, together as disciples, can respond in mutuality to the challenges facing our communities and world.

In addition, our efforts at mission education must be undergirded by actual engagement in cross-cultural relationships, whether traveling internationally to visit partners in Africa, Asia, or Latin America; hosting international partners in North America; or working with African, Asian, or Latin American churches locally in our own context. It has been said that "it is easier to act someone into a different way of thinking than to think someone into a different way of acting." Unless the educational efforts we make are related to real person-to-person relationships, we have no way of putting our new perceptions into action. Furthermore, we can only truly understand our new perceptions when we are willing to engage and learn from others.

Power or powerlessness (depending on where you are) is a phenomenon that has been internalized over centuries. Some church visitors still come to countries in Africa, Asia, or Latin America because they have read a biased history that speaks about heroic missionaries like David Livingstone. They come as "heroes" and "heroines" to help people whom they see as helpless. On the other hand, others still see themselves as "helpless," like the man at the pool of Bethsaida (John 5:1–16), who need things done for them. Transforming this understanding requires a radical program of relationship building and immersion experiences alongside curriculum development and study, undertaken together by partners in the South and North.

Mission should be about the capacity to receive as we give. Jesus was not just someone who cared, taught, and gave to others. He also learned from others and was cared for by his friends, such as Lazarus and his sisters, Simon the leper, and the woman with the expensive perfume. How does the church in North America receive from the Global South? How does the church in North America learn from partners, and how are beliefs and theologies influenced by our friends in the South?

Ultimately, mission in the twenty-first century must follow God's call to humanize relationships. We must grow in our ability to demonstrate to the world that we can truly live as brothers and sisters beyond race, culture, gender, and other boundaries. In essence, mission involves the capacity to live and learn together and, in the process, understand in deeper and new ways what it means to be truly human.

QUESTIONS FOR STUDY AND DIALOGUE

1. What does partnership mean to you? In what ways have your understandings changed?

2. If partnership has been so problematic in the past, how can we today hope to experience life-giving relationships in which there is true mutuality—receiving and sharing on all sides?

3. How does the church in North America receive from the global South? How can we learn from partners, and how are our theologies influenced by our friends in the South?

2

MISSION IN A GLOBALIZED WORLD

Beverly Eileen Mitchell

THE TRIUNE GOD—Parent, Son, and Holy Spirit—is missional. The missional activity of the church is God's work and is grounded in the nature of the triune God, who is relational, expansive, and dynamic. The challenge of Christian mission in the twenty-first century is to discern how churches can participate in this task in the context of globalization and religious pluralism in a world deeply fractured by economic injustice, continuous war, unmitigated violence, dehumanizing patterns of discrimination, religious extremism, civil and political unrest, and environmental disruption. This chapter will explore what it means to say that global mission is God's work, articulate some of the ways in which mission is grounded in the nature of God, and identify implications for engagement in mission in today's global context.

MISSION AS GOD'S WORK

The doctrine of the Trinity is an important grounding for how we have come to understand the nature of mission today. Although the word "trinity" is never mentioned in the Bible, the church in history has affirmed the triune nature of God. To affirm God as triune is not to assert that there are three gods. Rather, this means that in ways that promote salvation, God has manifested God's self as Parent, Son, and Holy Spirit in the work of creating, redeeming, and sustaining the world. Each member of the Trinity is eternally and co-equally involved in this work and they are completely at one. At the same time, they are distinct in the manner in which they engage in their relationships with humans and creation. This harmonious fellowship of love within the Trinity, characterized by mutuality and reciprocity, suggests that the very nature of the triune God is communal, relational, and dynamic. Through the Son, Jesus Christ, this fellowship embraces humanity and draws us into the very life of God.

The mission of God is the source and basis for the mission of the church. Christian churches have come to recognize that they have no mission of their own. God has been at work within the entire human race and the whole of creation throughout history. Even before we have engaged in any missional activity, God has been present and active. Our participation in mission involves working openly for right relationships with fellow human beings and with the rest of creation. In a real sense, mission is not what the church does in addition to other activities; rather, all other activities of the church arise from the principal task of mission.

The mission of the church involves two principal activities that are interconnected. Both activities constitute the nature of our participation in God's work in the world. If either activity is missing from the missional enterprise, our participation in God's work is inadequate. First, the church is sent into the world to bear witness to the saving act of God in Jesus Christ. The church calls the world to repentance, announces the forgiveness of sin, and heralds the inauguration of a new beginning in relations with God and with our neighbors through Jesus Christ. Second, the church announces the in-breaking of the reign of God, which is a radical movement of God toward humanity and creation. As a result of the inauguration of God's realm, the church is called to reflect, individually and corporately, the transformation we seek in God's world. To the extent that we are faithful in prophetic witness against social structures, beliefs, and practices that deny the physical, emotional, and spiritual well-being of all people, we testify to the provisional presence of God's reign. (Christians recognize that though the reign of God was inaugurated through the life, ministry, death, and resurrection of Christ, it is not yet present in all its fullness.)

MISSION IS RELATIONAL

Christian mission is relational, for it arises out of the very nature of God, who is relational. A principal element of the divine embrace entails reconciliation—restoring right relationships—between God and humanity and all of creation. Through the work of the Holy Spirit, as the bond of love between God and the Son, human beings are wooed toward sacred communion with the God of love. God's purpose for all human beings is that our love for God and each other mirrors the harmonious fellowship that exists between the members of the Trinity. The presence of agape love is the principal way in which others, inside and outside of our churches, can discern whether we are true followers of Christ (John 13:35). The presence of the fruit of the Spirit (Gal. 5:22–23), an outgrowth of the redemptive work of Jesus Christ, is indispensable in equipping us to meet the demands of mission within our churches and beyond. Our churches are communities of faith in which all members are to support and encourage each other to discover their gifts and ministries. In turn, these gifts are given to be used for the edification of those within the community and ministry beyond the walls of our churches. Every member is equipped in some way to play a role in Christian mission. In sharing the gospel with others, we color the credibility of our message by the degree to which we engage in the practice of radical hospitality within our churches. Opening our doors to strangers, to the poor, and to social outcasts are concrete expressions of faithful discipleship and living under God's reign.

To say Christian mission is relational is to affirm the importance of the quality of the relationships between local and global churches. To experience the fullness of the mission movement of the Holy Spirit, we need to be part of the local witness of our churches and also connected to the church globally. In times of economic uncertainty it can be difficult to determine whether and to what extent we should concentrate our resources on the needs of our local communities and contribute to the deeply pressing needs of those far beyond our borders. Such tensions are not new, but they seem more acute in our time.

We must keep in mind that the church's commitment to mission is a call to recognize that there is only one mission and that local and global mission engagement are two aspects of the same vocation. Both are needed and they safeguard the well-being of each other. We are called to engage in the work of sharing the gospel at home and among people beyond our borders. This must be a cooperative effort, without competition for resources, which reflects the unity of purpose to which Christ's disciples have been called. Mission domestically, with a proven record of transformation of lives on the home front, can offer credibility for mission abroad. Domestic ministries can also provide both personnel and finances that can assist in mission on a global scale. Vital mission efforts locally can lead to the accumulation of a wealth of experiences in sharing the gospel that can be successfully contextualized in other places. Likewise, when domestic mission connects with the larger global context, it serves to remind everyone that no locale, no church, no denomination "owns" the gospel, for God's good news is intended to be liberating and life-affirming for all people.

Moreover, cross-cultural engagement in missional activity provides opportunities for participants to serve each other, gain new perspectives, and aid in the vitality that can arise from the cross-fertilization of ideas and life experiences. Churches must seek fellowship with other churches beyond their doors and beyond their borders as an expression of the oneness in Christ that binds all Christians. Fellowship can be characterized by mutuality and reciprocity between smaller and larger churches; established churches and new church plants; and Protestant, Orthodox, and Catholic churches. Wherever this participation in the Spirit's work of support, sustenance, and renewal in the world is present, God is glorified.

We live in a world where different ethnicities, cultures, religions, and languages rub shoulders each day. This context is referred to as pluralism. Being relational in ways that foster mutuality and reciprocity is a particular challenge in the context of religious pluralism. Because of increased migration, religious pluralism is not limited to traditional regions of multifaith societies, such as those in Africa, Asia, and other parts of the world. Rather, religious pluralism has become a global reality. In some places Christians, and those of other faith traditions, enjoy freedom and are privileged to live in cooperation with others in a spirit of mutual respect and understanding. However, in other regions, for a multitude of reasons, religious intolerance is strong and makes it difficult to cultivate relationships of trust. Christians and others have been guilty of attitudes of intolerance and violence in the past and, in some places, even today. Although Christians in historically multifaith societies have over the centuries gained experience in how to witness in such contexts, even these communities have not escaped new challenges as the world, through globalization, grows smaller. Christian methods of sharing the gospel, locally or globally, should always be governed by the ways in which God relates to us; namely, in the spirit of love, without coercion, in a manner that acknowledges the freedom of human beings to accept or reject God's invitation of reconciliation. God is at work both inside and outside the churches in ways that surprise us as to the magnitude of God's grace and mercy toward all. Furthermore, we are encouraged to cultivate relationships where meaningful dialogue helps to foster understanding and facilitates cooperative engagement in urgent local and global issues that affect human beings and the rest of creation.

MISSION IS EXPANSIVE

God's mission is also expansive. Mission is not only sharing the salvation story nor is it solely sharing financial resources. Mission includes active engagement in the task of promoting the work of justice in God's world for the sake of the restoration of all things in heaven and earth in Jesus Christ. This means that the gospel is good news for every part of creation

16 | THE CURRENT CONTEXT OF MISSION

and every aspect of our lives. If we proclaim the good news of the presence of the reign of God in our midst, then those who receive this news with joy are called to live consistently with the values of that reign. The good news is more than the salvation of individual human "souls." The good news encompasses the liberation of all creation. The recognition of the expansive nature of mission has huge implications for how we relate not only to human beings but to the rest of creation as well.

Proclamation of the gospel of Jesus Christ is a liberating mission, particularly in contexts where segments of our populations are pushed to the margins through exclusionary practices that bar them from full participation in our societies. Racism, sexism, caste discrimination, xenophobia, marginalization of persons with disabilities, forced migration, and criminalization of the poor (to name only a few) infect not only our societies, but our local and global churches as well. We cannot proclaim the liberating activity of God in Jesus Christ on one hand, and ignore the ways in which such cultural biases infect not only our societies, but even our churches, on the other hand.

Mission empowered by the Holy Spirit includes the task of bearing witness against economic, social, cultural, and political structures that abuse, exploit, and dehumanize the vulnerable. Whenever we engage in the task of bearing witness, our actions become concrete expressions of the reality of the reign of God in our midst. Such witness includes the persistent affirmation of the dignity and worth of every man, woman, and child, because each has been created in the image of God and is invited to receive the redemption offered in Jesus Christ. To engage in the prophetic dimension of Christian mission underscores our active partnership with God, who seeks to transform our relationships from unjust ones to just ones.

The prophetic task of mission obligates us to affirm the sacredness of human life and responsible stewardship of the environment and nonhuman creatures. To remain faithful to this dimension of mission affirms the integrity of our proclamation of God's good news. Transformation of our relationships expands beyond the divine-human and human-human contexts to include the human-creation context as well. As we seek to understand more fully the causes of climate change and human responsibility for environmental disturbances that adversely affect air quality, fresh water supply, and the availability of arable land, we have become keenly aware of our profound interdependence with all living things. The well-being of human beings, nonhuman creatures, and the environment is dependent upon our making a conscious commitment to safeguard life in all its forms.

Our acts of bearing witness to the Holy Spirit's working against injustice among the marginalized and against disregard for the welfare of creation are part of the mission of God in which we are called to participate. These acts are expressions of faithful discipleship, which testify to the ways in which Christ's disciples express genuine love of neighbor and responsible care for the good creation.

MISSION IS DYNAMIC

Because the triune God we love and serve is dynamic, not static, our mission activity must be dynamic, too. Methods of mission engagement employed in the past may not work as effectively in our current context or time. This makes discernment as to what God is doing in our midst today essential. In the third millennium, Christianity has reemerged as a global religion again. The missionary efforts of Christ's disciples in the first century contributed to the global expansion of Christianity in North Africa, Western Asia, Iraq, Iran, and other places. The evangelistic efforts of Christians in Africa, Asia, and Latin America in the nineteenth and twentieth centuries have contributed to the globalization of Christianity today.

In the last century and a half, Western Europe and North America were perceived as critical centers of influence in modern Christianity. However, by the close of the twentieth century, Christianity in Europe and, to some extent, North America declined. The influence and vibrancy of Christianity have become more pronounced in the very regions that were formerly the recipients of massive missionary efforts. There are no

18 | THE CURRENT CONTEXT OF MISSION

longer one or two major centers of evangelistic activity; now there are many centers. Moreover, the major regions of growth in the number of adherents to Christianity are now in Africa, Latin America, Asia, and the Pacific Islands. The multiple centers of mission activity in our time reflect that God's work cannot be domesticated nor does any people or region of the world—not even the churches—own or monopolize the movement of the Holy Spirit engaged in enlivening, nurturing, and equipping peoples in the work of saving the world and all therein.

In the last century, churches have come to a greater understanding that the Christian faith takes hold in specific human cultures. This speaks to the reality that the gospel itself is incarnational—the Word of God becomes concrete in local cultures in particularized ways. This means that no culture exemplifies the sum measure for the expression of the nature of God's relationship with human communities. Authentic faith communities emerge to the extent that the gospel is free to engage fully within the culture it encounters.

While in the last two hundred years the missionary enterprise took place within the sociopolitical context of a vast expansion of colonization, now mission activity occurs within the context of socioeconomic globalization. A critical aspect of globalization is the unlimited flow of capital all over the world under the direction of transnational corporations that seek to attain maximum profit in a short period of time. Economic considerations have become the major criteria for human interaction. In the global market, consumption of goods and services is highly prized, whether these goods and services are needed or not. Moreover, not everyone is able to enjoy access to the global economy in ways that promote human flourishing. The most vulnerable populations—the poor, the sick and disabled, the unemployed and underemployed—are excluded. Alongside the tragic consequences of this economic trend on human beings, globalization has contributed to the degradation of the environment. The exploitation of the earth's natural resources has resulted in ecological crises and disasters, which threaten the quality of life for everyone. Christianity is most vibrant in regions with populations most adversely affected by the impact of globalization.

What are the startling implications of the fact that the gospel is vital and growing in places of the world where the poorest of the poor can be found? Mission in the nineteenth century was often directed at peoples on the margins of societies, with the assumption that the marginalized could not be agents of missionary activity. As a result of Christianity's shift of influence to the Global South, those of us outside of that context are being shown important insights about God's activity in the world. Openness to hearing the voices of the marginalized have reminded us that Christ identified most with the outcasts, the despised, and the forsaken. Because Christ chose to make common cause with such groups (Matt. 25:31–46), we are invited to perceive the ways in which the Holy Spirit is leading them now.

These changes in the context of mission suggest the need for churches to evaluate their methods of evangelism to ensure that the proclamation of the gospel is received as good news. But these changing contexts also provide Christian communities opportunity—the opportunity to build upon those aspects of their efforts that have borne fruit, so as to develop methods of discernment of the Holy Spirit's presence, methods that bring gratitude to those who find their liberation in the proclamation of Christ. The exciting challenge of mission in this dynamic context lies in discovering the ways in which local and global churches can discern how God is already at work. By entering into relationships characterized by mutual respect, cooperation, and reciprocity, those involved in mission at multiple levels can acquire new perspectives on God's mission in the world.

QUESTIONS FOR STUDY AND DIALOGUE

1. If the two principal activities of the mission of the church are (1) to bear witness to the saving act of God in Jesus Christ and (2) to announce the in-breaking of the reign of God, how well does your local church maintain the balance between these two activities? If this balance is not well-maintained, how might your congregation begin to work toward engaging both?

20 | THE CURRENT CONTEXT OF MISSION

2. In what ways might local churches in your community strengthen their relationships with each other, in order to contribute to genuine fellowship?

3. What steps do you believe local churches could take to cultivate relationships with churches in other parts of the world?

4. In what ways can more materially affluent congregations foster more mutually supportive relationships with less affluent congregations, locally and globally?

5. What are some of the concrete ways your local church can practice faithful stewardship of the earth's resources?

II | NURTURING COMMUNITY

3

RECEIVING IN PARTNERSHIP
Opening Our Hearts

Gloria Vicente Canú, Phyllis Byrd, Susan McNeely;
Catherine Nichols, *editor*

THIS CHAPTER INCLUDES three stories of partnership and of how, as we deepen connections, we receive more than we give. Gloria, Phyllis, and Susan are women with deep connections to Global Ministries; each tells her story of acting as the bridge between our local North American churches and the life and Christian witness of our partners. As missionaries, they share their understandings of the challenge of real partnership and how open eyes, ears, and hearts can allow us to truly live as one in the body of Christ.

After church on Sunday, there are some hymns that stay in your head for days. Their passages come back as you sweep the floor or drive down the road. One such hymn that continues to resonate long into the week is an amazing expression of how we must change to truly be open to witnessing God:

Open my eyes that I may see
glimpses of truth thou hast for me

This hymn, "Open My Eyes" (Clara H. Scott, 1895), can become a silent prayer for understanding when a situation is new or challenging. In the first story of the transition of partnership in today's world, Gloria Vicente Canu, a missionary serving in Guatemala, shares the ways in which we have had to change how we view mission to live truly into partnership. As our eyes have opened to seeing, we are called into authentic relationship—because anything less than that does not recognize our common presence as a child of God.

Open my ears that I may hear
voices of truth thou sendest clear

The second story of relationship comes from our missionary in Kenya, Phyllis Byrd. As she witnesses the growing connections—and occasional misconnections—between our churches and our partners, she asks us to open our ears and hear the stories from our partners, to receive the message of the drum calling for community and right relations with one another.

Open my mind that I may read
more of thy love in word and deed

The final story comes from Susan McNeely, who served as a volunteer in the Democratic Republic of the Congo. Although we often think of what we give when we volunteer—our time and our treasure—Susan reminds us that what we receive in return is so much more. With the opportunity to know God's people in all corners of the earth, our own faith is challenged, strengthened, and renewed.

WEAVING A NEW MODEL
Gloria Vicente Canú

"Truth, according to the Christian faith, is God's love for us in Jesus Christ. Therefore, truth is a relationship" (Pope Francis).[1]

The Mayan people of Guatemala weave together elaborate threads worked on a back-strap loom to create true works of art passed down from generation to generation. Through authentic patterns and colors, these threads express a thousand-year-old history woven together into one worldview. This worldview has undergirded the contemporary Mayan communities' struggle for self-determination, for their rights and identities. They have endured hundreds of years of colonialism, from the Spanish invasion to today's neocolonialism by those who wish to exploit the land and its resources. As people called today to join in God's mission, we must move beyond old understandings and patterns of mission practiced in the past. We are challenged to participate in constructive processes and to practice authenticity in everything we do, in terms of how we serve in our ministries today. We must reflect genuine commitment and intentions within the context of partnerships.

In practice, authenticity is a truthful way of answering God's call to serve and accompany partners globally and of understanding accompaniment (walking side by side) as a mutual need. This is a need that goes beyond our long historic view of the "us/them" dichotomy that has engendered racist, exclusive, and isolated views and practices throughout much of our church's history. The challenge is to transform these views and practices into interdependent actions where North–South/South–North relationships are based on respect, truth, and ethical and authentic relationships that nurture Christ's teachings of discipleship, fellowship, and stewardship.

Partnerships, however, are not always authentic. Through faulty partnerships, we risk succumbing to a hesitancy to repeat historical mistakes and, by doing this, risk doing more harm to brothers and sisters abroad. Mission today requires self-examination as an institution that serves others in mission. Our institutional mission statement should lead us to reflect on the critical need to address how and for how long we participate in carrying out God's mission globally. We should immediately and repeatedly ask ourselves if we are truthfully abiding by that mission statement and "meeting God's people and creation at the point of deepest need" and receiving and sharing the good news of Jesus Christ through current mission-driven acts of active solidarity, especially as we stand with our partners in the midst of political, environmental, religious, economic, and social conflicts. Furthermore, we must question if we have in any way deviated from this stated intention and thus become yet another charity-based organization, simply distributing funds without nurturing the relationships.

If the answer is that we have started down the charity path, we need to rally as a wider church in efforts to build strong and authentic partnerships not based on charity, but on mutual accompaniment and witness. It means building capacity through partnerships as opposed to short-lived handouts. In a broken world, today, more than ever, each church must be proactive and stand in mutual support and compassion with churches and like-minded partners abroad.

As missionaries, we are appointed to work with partners in capacity-building processes that focus on leadership and community development. When invited, we are called to participate and contribute to the construction of authentic relationships where our partners, our ministries, and the communities we serve can feel accompanied and empowered as opposed to being isolated or disregarded. The Mayan Kaqchikel women's textile arts project exemplifies this type of authentic partnership. This project allows women who experience triple discrimination for being female, indigenous, and economically disadvantaged to reclaim their identity by learning and rescuing ancestral weaving practices. As a result, they actively participate in a process to reclaim their voices, to become proactive decision makers and active agents of change as well as entrepreneurs.

The formation of life-giving and affirming relationships is not without significant barriers and challenges. Often there are social barriers that hinder Mayan women's leadership roles, particularly as it pertains to the discrimination and marginalization that women face daily at home, in their community, and even among other women. As a missionary called to work with different indigenous women's communities, I have learned of the importance of holistic and culturally pertinent empowerment of women to facilitate the process for leadership development. In this context, holistic empowerment includes healing wounds stemming from a thirty-six-year-long civil war that left thousands of widows and inflicted upon them a psychological terror that today is expressed through distrust, fear, and a lack of voice and identity. In this project, a partnership was formed to support Mayan women's identity and empowerment, building from the general Mayan identity but focusing on traditional women's community contributions and power, based on a thousand-year-old history of weaving. Through this weaving process, women have resisted cultural colonialism and preserved a worldview through elaborate woven iconography. Within the context of the weaving arts project, empowerment comes from creating authentic working relationships built on trust and on fundamental values that include the realities of Mayan women and a process that is initiated, organized, carried out, and administered by women.

Other organizations rely on short-term projects carried out by outsiders within marginalized communities. Although the term "partnership" is often used to describe these relationships, more often than not these short-term and potentially exploitative projects have resulted in more harm, creating dependency, and have exhausted trust and consensus processes within communities. In the case of Mayan women, these disengaged models have perpetuated a continued marginalization and misrepresentation.

Like weavings that get old and worn out, so too do old models of thinking. There is a present need for us to rethread the loom, warping and weaving, wrapping and meshing threads together with new common ideas and visions. One example includes the important role of North American churches that participate in People to People Pilgrimages to partners, like in Guatemala, where they are able to participate in authentic and transformative relationships and processes. Through engagement, diversity, and participation as a wider Christian community, we can feel empowered collectively by sharing and witnessing testimonies of faith with partners at home and globally.

SHHHH . . . LISTEN TO THE BEAT OF THE DRUM
Phyllis Byrd

I recently received a challenging set of e-mails from a woman who had been on a mission trip to Kenya. Her last e-mail read: "And you have the nerve to call yourself a minister. The reason why there is so much famine and many other problems in your country is because I noticed when my church came to help your people on a mission trip, God was not central to the life of the country. This is why your country has so many problems."

And now I was in real pain. I had to think back to the visit of the mission team and ask myself, "Where did I go wrong?" Could the other members of the mission team think like her? Is it possible that the whole mission team missed the beat of the drum?

In many different cultures in Africa, the drum has deep and diverse symbolic meaning. The way the drum is beat conveys many different meanings. The drumbeat can be for a celebratory event such as a wedding or a birth. There is also a beat to announce a death in the community. There is another beat that unmasks evil in society. It exposes disharmony and injustice and drives it out of the community. There is another beat that resounds for miles, calling the whole community to a *Baraza*, a structured meeting or gathering of members in the community to reflect on community concerns. When the drum beats, all the community responds to the call regardless of their social, political, educational, or economic positions in the society. The community responds to the drum out of a common understanding that they are embedded with one another. When there is a breakdown in the society, it is not an individual concern but a collective problem that all must work on to restore harmony and justice.

I would like to believe that this individual who sent me the e-mail did not represent the sentiments of the whole mission team, but it raises a fundamental question of how we prepare ourselves to receive in mission. I get at least ten e-mails a year from mission teams planning a visit to Kenya or the East Africa region:

"The mission team is planning a mission trip to Kenya and East Africa and we would like to . . . [paint an orphanage or a school, build something, set up a medical camp, bring our choir to visit and share our gift of music, have our young people come and work at an orphanage for a few weeks, etc.]."

The generosity of the mission teams' time and financial commitments are commendable, but the effort to give can sometimes blind us from receiving the resourcefulness of the people we are visiting. We miss hearing the drumbeat when we consciously or unconsciously compare where we live with where we are going on mission. We can become deaf from the sound of the "old adding machines" as we subconsciously calculate our "privileged" positions, our resources, net worth, and possessions, while at the same time subconsciously recording on the ledger the lack of resources of those our mission team will visit. We give to them, we help, they receive; we go home feeling good and fulfilled.

"For you say, 'I am rich, I have prospered, and I need nothing.' You do not realize that you are wretched, pitiable, poor, blind, and naked . . ." (Rev. 3:17).

To receive in mission is to come with open hands, heart, mind, and spirit to meet a new set of friends. It is through genuine communion that we open ourselves to receive the resourcefulness of the family of God. To receive in mission is transformative reciprocity for those whom we visit as well as for the mission team. Mission teams are transformed as they encounter God in fresh and dynamic ways through the people they visit. Mission teams are changed as they acknowledge how poor in spirit we are and that our need to encounter God in fresh and new ways, as well as our critical need for new friends who see the world with different eyes, can only be met when we widen our circle of God's world. Our encounter should not be with poverty but with resourcefulness and the synergy of coming together as a liberating moment for all.

"This is my command: Love one another the way I loved you. This is the very best way to love. Put your life on the line for your friends. You are my friends when you do the things I command you. I'm no longer calling you servants because servants don't understand what their master is thinking and planning. No, I've named you friends . . ." (John 15:11–15 MSG).

This depth of the love that Jesus has for us, which causes him to call us a friend, is what we are commanded to reciprocate to others. I have experienced this organic love to which Jesus refers as it has been extended to mission teams that visit Kenya and the East Africa region.

There is a story illustrating this love found in the John 15:11–15. The general secretary of the Organization of Africa Instituted Churches, Rev. Nicta Lubaale, was traveling by road from Kenya to attend a meeting in Tanzania. He had an allergic infection, which caused his eyes to become red, so he had to wear sunglasses to protect his eyes. Upon reaching the boarder of Kenya and Tanzania there were women selling items to travelers crossing the border. This is how they make their living; it is a difficult life and most of them make only a few coins a day because of the competition from others selling. When Rev. Nicta's car approached the border crossing, he came out of the car to go to the immigration office. One of the women approached him with the items she was selling. He took off his glasses to greet her because culturally it would be rude for a younger man to greet an older woman wearing dark glasses. It is also culturally important that one makes eye contact with a person. When he took off his sunglasses after greeting her, the older woman said "Oh, sorry, your eyes are sick."

She put down her wares on the side of the road and turned her attention to his "sick eyes." She wanted to hear Rev. Nicta's story of why his eyes were sick and what he was doing to get better. She made suggestions of what he could do to be well and avoid his eyes becoming sick again. This older woman, who makes her living selling things on the side of the road, was willing to put aside her economic livelihood to assist someone who was sick. The woman he encountered stopped looking for money for her daily bread in order to hear what the problem was with Rev. Nicta, who was a stranger before they encountered each other. A transformation took place, and now he was her son. Rev. Nicta became part of her when she turned her attention to him. All of her efforts were focused on his well-being.

We receive in mission as we listen. Come with open hands and arms to receive from the resourcefulness of those with whom we seek to share. We receive in mission as we put aside our interest and open ourselves to see our own poverty. We receive in mission when we take the time to listen and to encounter the stranger; it is through such an encounter that we are transformed into friends. We receive in mission as we quiet ourselves and listen to the drumbeat.

RECEIVING IN MISSION
Susan McNeely

This story starts many years ago when, fresh out of seminary and graduate school, my husband and I accepted a call from the Protestant Church in Belgium to help it reach U.S. citizens living in areas of Belgium where English-speaking churches were not readily available. During those two years, our mentors and the Christians we encountered taught us much about life, faith, and what it means to welcome the stranger in your midst. The impact of this experience was life-changing—so much so that it took several years for us to completely readjust to life in the United States when we returned. It was then that I first learned how a mission experience could so profoundly impact those who served that they can never truly go back to their previous lives. They are literally transformed in a way that is not possible in their home culture, and their future will be very different than it would have been had they not accepted the call. My life was so enriched by living among the Belgians and my worldview so radically expanded that I would seek out opportunities to serve and be served again and again.

So it went for many years; as I worked and raised a family, I managed to carve out time to study the church in Nepal, help rebuild a city destroyed by a hurricane, build houses in Honduras and El Salvador, and do various projects in Appalachia and on a Native American reservation. I knew that I needed to be outside my own comfort zone in order to grow, to receive the Spirit in a way that could not happen at home. Although each of these experiences was referred to as a mission trip, they were more like pilgrimages. The work was always peripheral to the opportunity to share our lives, to learn from those we came to serve, to see another face of God. I returned home humbled by the way people opened themselves to strangers, knowing inside that while I may have arrived a stranger, I left as a friend. There simply was no better way to find God than to look into the eyes of someone different than me.

Through the partnership formed between the Christian Church in Indiana and the Mbandaka Post of the 10th-Community Disciples of Christ in Congo, I made two separate trips to the Democratic Republic of the Congo and helped host our Congolese visitors on return trips to Indiana. Many hours were spent in pirogues, motorboats, and automobiles. Deep friendships were formed from the sharing that took place on these travels.

A time came in 2011 when our friends expressed a strong conviction that they needed to find a way to learn or improve their English, not only to communicate with us, but also to better tell their own stories in the global community through conferences and the Internet. I pondered how this could be accomplished. On their next visit to Indiana, I asked our friends what they thought about me coming for a short term "mission" to teach English as a foreign language. They were enthusiastic and the seeds were planted. Out of partnership came this strong call to do something that I knew would be difficult; however, I could find no reason to refuse. The work began. Gift upon gift arrived—dear friends in Mbandaka offered to host me in their new house; my home congregation donated money for a motorcycle so that there would be transportation while I was there; a friend, a skill-teacher, taught me how to plan a curriculum and deliver lessons—very important, since I had never really taught before.

There is no question that this was one of the hardest things I have ever done. Planning and preparation took months; health precautions had to be observed; the travel to Mbandaka is long and arduous; daily life in Congo is never simple or easy; the weather was hot; materials for classes were only what I could create myself. From the very beginning, though, it felt as if Jesus was standing by my side—sometimes in the guise of my hosts, my students, or church members who dropped by with a pineapple, an avocado, an egg. Visits to churches meant coming home with a large sack of food (plus an occasional chicken, fish, or crocodile) to help feed me during my stay. It took a major effort to accept the attention and the gifts gracefully, knowing that they were given from people who also struggled daily to provide the basics of life. One of the best gifts was the lesson that I had to allow partners to serve me, day in and day out, because I could not function without their help. Humility comes hard to a privileged person. One student came five hundred miles by motorcycle and canoe and stayed three months, just for the opportunity to attend our humble classes. How can you ever find a way to offer something worthy of that kind of dedication? I received, and received, and received, until the day I left the country. Most of all, for three months, my hosts shared their lives with me, and we are forever linked.

The gifts continue. Besides answering a request from our partners, I had a very intentional second goal to help North Americans know more about the struggles faced by the Congolese so that we might find ways to stand in solidarity with them. I discovered on my return that many people had been following my journey and praying for my safety and success while I was gone. Women of Oregon and western Idaho graciously extended an invitation for me to share my story, and they shared their stories with me. Again, pushed way outside my comfort zone, I received a blessing.

The simple lesson I have learned through mission engagement is this: The work that is done, the good that is accomplished, will always be secondary to the encounter with other children of God. Understanding that

34 | NURTURING COMMUNITY

the best gift you have is your own heart enables you to receive the love that is offered by those with whom you seek to serve.

QUESTIONS FOR STUDY AND DIALOGUE

1. Why should you choose to put yourself in an unfamiliar, and perhaps uncomfortable, situation from time to time?

2. What does it mean to serve, and to be served?

3. Where have you encountered God today?

4

RELATIONSHIPS
Why and How We Serve in Mission

Elena Huegel, Judy Chan, Jeffrey Mensendiek;
Catherine Nichols, *editor*

THIS CHAPTER INCLUDES three stories of relationships—and how forging those relationships can lead us into the true depth of missional service. Elena, Judy, and Jeff are three experienced missionaries with Global Ministries, and each tells a story from their years of service. They share their understanding of the bonds that come with the gift of time, of what it means to have an open heart, and the recognition that service often benefits those sent as much as or more than those who receive.

Theologically, we can start this chapter with the story of the good Samaritan. In the traditional concept of mission, we jump to this story of missionaries as the good Samaritans—the ones who stop, see the wounded, and assist. But mission within the context of deep relationship is not that simple, nor, as Christians from North America, are our roles with partners. Sometimes we arrive as the high priest who walks by and does nothing, especially if we come to a partner with our own solutions to problems we may not understand—like the visiting youth in Elena's

36 | NURTURING COMMUNITY

piece. Sometimes in mission, as Judy shares, we are the road—we create space for the community to carry forward its own efforts. And sometimes, as Jeff eloquently describes, we may be the man beaten on the side of the road, and, through our participation in mission, we are carried forward as we see and experience the new face of Christ.

CLIPPING FOR CHRIST
Elena Huegel

"Clip, clip, clippity, clip" go the pruning shears in the hands of an energetic and bright teenager from the United States during an intercultural peace-building camp at the Shalom Center of the Pentecostal Church of Chile. She has signed up for trail maintenance while other members of her delegation have volunteered to paint, dig a hole for the septic tank, or make wooden tables for the outdoor dining area with teens from a local church in Chile. The trail keepers at the Shalom Center battle all summer with the blackberry bushes and wild roses that grow three to five inches a day, threatening to take over the trails and choke out the natural underbrush. These invasive species were brought to Chile from Spain at the time of the conquest to make natural fence lines. The cows, goats, and sheep that eat the berries and rosehips have helped to seed the bushes throughout the native forests of central Chile.

At the end of the first day, sweaty, scratched, and somewhat discouraged with the never-ending berry battle, the trail keepers seek me out. "We have been thinking about quicker, easier, and better ways to get rid of the berries and roses," they exclaim excitedly. "Why don't we burn the bushes?" I pause, searching carefully for an answer because I want to encourage creative problem solving along with reflection on the consequences of different proposals. "That would certainly be quicker. How would we keep the whole forest from going up in flames?" We talk about why the berry and rose bushes in other areas have flourished after a burn. Could it be that the soil was enriched or that there was more sunlight after the burn? "We might use a weed killer to get rid of the plants," one suggests, but the others argue about the dangers of pesticide use. Could the chemicals be applied to each individual bush in the exact amounts to kill the roots without damaging the native weeds or poisoning water sources?

Finally, I share with the group a recommendation from the forest biologists at a nearby university: Protect the local flora so that in fifty or sixty years the invasive species die off when the native trees and bushes block out the sunlight. The teens, with renewed energy, conclude: "While we wait for nature to finish the job, we must keep the berry and rose bushes at bay and care for the native growth as best we can. Our small efforts today are part of a healthier forest in the future!"

Why take the long road in God's mission through collaboration and mutuality when there seem to be so many "quicker, easier, and better" ways to "fix" the problems of the world? The berry and rose bushes planted by the Spaniards were a quick fix to the fencing problem in an open expanse of new territory, and we are still dealing with the consequences of that solution centuries later. Our mission, as well as our earth-care efforts, have often been like the planting of the berry and rose bushes. We have started projects and programs believing we knew exactly what was needed without exploring local wisdom or fully measuring the long-term results of our actions.

One important reason for deepening our relationships, recognizing our interdependence and reaching across cultural and language differences while working for the Lord of the harvest is precisely to slow us down. In our North American "buy now, pay later" rush to consume, while believing that somehow new technologies will save us from any disaster we happen to create in the process, our sisters and brothers in other parts of the world remind us that our role in God's mission is to be workers in God's garden, cultivating and restoring right relationships with God, ourselves, others, and all of creation. Ephesians 4:2–6 asks us to work together, "with all humility and gentleness, with patience, bearing with one another in love, making every effort to maintain the unity of the Spirit in the bond of peace." As God's gardeners we must slow down: renewing the soil, sowing the seeds, weeding, and waiting faithfully for the riches of our growing relationships to bear good and lasting fruit.

The purpose of the Shalom Center in Chile is to create a safe space where people can come together to explore ways of cultivating and restoring right relationships. Every year, when new volunteers in the "trail keeper" crew return from the first day of clipping, they complain about the hard work, long walks, hot sun, and gnarled masses of thorns. Every year, after clearing another bit of the underbrush or opening up a trail for the enjoyment of others, they become a tight-knit group. Nature treats them with surprises no one else at camp enjoys: a new view of the Andes Mountains, a fox startled from its hiding place, a snake hidden in the bushes. At camp, their different pasts become one trail of stories, laughs, struggles, and shared memories. After a week away from cell phones, computers, and the Internet, technology serves to support their newly built relationships: Facebook, Skype, and WhatsApp become ways to stay connected and share pictures, dreams, and prayer needs.

At nature's invitation to simplicity, the mutual experiences of cold showers, no electricity, close quarters, bug bites, and fine volcano dust, which permeates everything from shoes to nostrils, prepare the participants and staff at the Shalom Center to become a community with faith, dignity, creativity, and the safe space for transformation at its core. Together we strive for that "wisdom from above," which "is first pure, then peaceable, gentle, willing to yield, full of mercy and good fruits, without a trace of partiality or hypocrisy" because we dream of a "harvest of righteousness . . . sown in peace for those who make peace" (James 3:17–18). We are the laborers that the Lord of the harvest is preparing to bring in a harvest of shalom (Matt. 9:38). Our patient efforts today are part of restored relationships with God, ourselves, others, and creation in the future!

CROSSING BOUNDARIES AND TAKING RISKS TO CONNECT
Judy Chan

From my experience in Hong Kong, I would like to share three lessons I have learned in developing effective and long-lasting relationships with our global partners in mission.

Serving with a Spirit of Humility

When I arrived at the Hong Kong Christian Council in 1994, my job assignment was clear. I was to set up a communications network with churches around the world in the run-up to 1997, when Hong Kong would return to the People's Republic of China. My job title, however, was interesting: "Special Assistant to the General Secretary." The general secretary, Dr. Tso Man-King, explained that he wanted to be sensitive to the other staff since I was coming from outside Hong Kong. Although I was qualified to carry the title of executive secretary, he created a new title so I would not be viewed as "above" or "below" any other staff in terms of rank, especially the other women. I didn't have a problem with that. It also alerted me to be sensitive to what image I projected with the partner, given its long missionary and colonial history. Eventually after a few years, the staff themselves decided I should be "promoted" to executive secretary. I agreed to take the title knowing that we had earned each other's trust and respect.

The need to embody a humble spirit and servant heart is essential in mission. That is true not only for partner church relationships but even more for the general community. The image of high-flying, well-to-do expatriates living a life of privilege is common in Hong Kong. It really makes an impression when the public sees foreigners who live a modest lifestyle on par with ordinary citizens as ambassadors for Christ. Even more important, though, is the willingness to be of service for whatever is needed as long as one is qualified or willing to learn. I never expected to be a radio producer. In fact, when I watched the person who had the position before me, I said, "Wow, I'm glad that's not my job!" But someone was needed to take up the role after the person retired, and, through the grace of God, I learned how to do it. I feel blessed that the broadcasting ministry can continue because of the presence of Global Ministries.

Working for God's Justice

Some mainline U.S. churches have a strong emphasis on justice and peace in their mission. How do we translate that prophetic call into action in other cultures? Fortunately for Hong Kong, there was a passionate, though small, network of Christians who were active in social justice concerns when I arrived. At the same time, these activists viewed the partner agency where I worked with suspicion due to a past history of conflicts. It was sometimes uncomfortable to be seen as working for the "bad guys" when I thought we were the good guys. Nevertheless, it was an opportunity to experience the challenges of the ecumenical movement firsthand.

Gratefully, we have made some progress over the years. Given the heated political environment of many of the places where Global Ministries has a presence, a missionary needs to proceed with caution under the guidance of the partner agency. We are there at the request of the partner, and also as a guest of the host church and country. As guests, we can make a difference by using our position strategically as an outsider who brings different perspectives and resources to bear on difficult situations. If nothing else, we might be more easily forgiven for our mistakes, given the assumption that we are naïve or ignorant! In reality, as Global Ministries missionaries, we have both an insider and outsider view, which can be valuable in formulating a more objective perspective on controversial political and social issues. However, I always keep in mind that I may have my own unacknowledged biases and that my American identity can easily be perceived as an unwelcome foreign (Western) influence, even if I don't think I have so much power.

Seeking Opportunities for Reconciliation

In the pursuit of peace and justice, I have seen how missionaries can play a pivotal role in bringing attention to neglected groups and advocating for their human rights and dignity. My own contribution in Hong Kong has been much more modest, yet I am grateful for opportunities to bring reconciliation in a couple of instances where there was terrible conflict that threatened to blow up into chaos.

One situation was in a church where the two parties could not agree on use of space. The other was between two agencies that served the same population but disagreed on policies and procedures. It was interesting that both cases involved working with marginalized groups in Hong Kong. Because of training I had received in conflict resolution long ago (and thought I would never use), I was able to work behind the scenes with one or both sides to break the deadlock. Of course, it wasn't just me—there were lots of other good people involved—but someone needed to help them change the toxic atmosphere. I was humbled that God had put me in a position to be a facilitator of reconciliation (in one case) and at least cessation of legal battles (in the other case).

Those incidents reminded me that reconciliation is at the heart of the gospel. And this reconciliation needs to start within the Christian community, which is often the hardest place to make it happen. We need to pray for an outpouring of the Holy Spirit again and again and trust God to bring healing and harmony when human efforts fail.

BEING THERE FOR ONE ANOTHER WHEN IT COUNTS
Jeff Mensendiek

In March of 2011, northeastern Japan was hit by a sizable earthquake registering a 9.0 on the Richter scale. The tsunami that followed wiped out villages and claimed countless lives. On the following day, nuclear plants in Fukushima started to explode. Those of us living in the area lost access to electricity, gas, and water. Cell phones didn't work. Food items were scarce and no gasoline was to be had at the gas stand. At night, our city of one million was pitch dark and life as we knew it came to a standstill. I think we all learned one important fact about life through this experience. When all life support systems are lost, relationships are what remain. At a time of crisis, the presence of another person and the relationships that we have nurtured through the years make all the difference.

I had been working at the Emmaus Center in Sendai, Japan, for more than twenty years with our partner, the United Church of Christ in Japan (UCCJ). After the disaster, the Emmaus Center became a relief center, and we began receiving volunteers from all over Japan to send out to the coast. At the same time, we were deeply aware of the unfolding nuclear crisis, conscious that neither the Japanese government nor the Tokyo Electric Company was on top of the situation. Soon the people that I worked with had an emergency evacuation manual ready for distribution. An emergency e-mail/fax system was also put in place to inform our churches in case of further troubles at the nuclear plants. Those first months were intense. We were trying to provide services to the wider public while at the same time regain a sense of balance in our own lives.

In the midst of this confusion, one of my colleagues, a young Japanese pastor, hopped on his bicycle to head down to the coast. It took him forty minutes to reach an elementary school that was serving as a temporary shelter for tsunami survivors. There he met a survivor, a carpenter named Mr. Sugawara. As they were talking, the pastor said, "Mr. Sugawara, we are looking for hope. We want to share this hope with our young people. Would you help us?" The pastor was thinking of the many volunteers who would be coming to help through the Emmaus Center. He wanted to make contact with a local person. He also knew that it was not going to be easy to gain the trust of the local people—especially if he was open about the fact that he was a Christian.

Sometimes it is hard for Christian folks in the United States to imagine what it is like to be a distinct minority within society. The church in Japan is small. Christians amount to less than one percent of the population. Average attendance at church on Sundays is twenty. You might ask yourself, "How do they manage to be the church with such small numbers?" In my eyes, the church in Japan is a miracle in itself. The Christians in Japan challenge our preconceptions of what it means to be the church. They face many challenges and hardships on account of their faith. The dominant culture often keeps a distance from Christianity, thinking that religious people are always out to proselytize.

Mr. Sugawara was no exception. Though he agreed to take our volunteers into the devastated area to help, he warned us, "I speak for our village when I say we don't like Christians and we don't care for volunteers." This, however, was the beginning of a beautiful relationship with the villagers of Shichigo. Today the villagers say to us, "Thank you, Emmaus Center. If it were not for you, we would not be where we are today."

I often marvel at the beautiful way in which the Japanese pastor entered into a relationship with the survivor. He did not go in saying, "How may I help you?" He did just the opposite. He found a local leader and asked, "Would you help us?" The survivors had lost everything and yet they had not lost their sense of dignity. The pastor's request was in effect saying, "Please lead us to hope. We will not find hope until you find hope." I think all of us were desperately looking for hope during those first months after the disaster, and in that sense we were all searching together. I discovered that true hope comes through mutual relationships of trust—when we look each other in the eye and say, "I have hope because of you."

A second powerful witness by our partners in Japan comes from a small church in Fukushima. Rev. Sasaki ministers to his flock of ten members in the village of Kashima, only thirty kilometers north of the reactors. After the nuclear plant explosions, Rev. Sasaki declared that he was not going to evacuate. We all questioned the wisdom of his decision.

Two years later, I had the opportunity to visit Rev. Sasaki in Kashima. I asked him about his decision to stay in the village. This is what he had to tell me:

"We all know it's dangerous here. There are no children left in the village. All who are left are the elderly, the handicapped, and the farmers. I feel their eyes on me and I know that they respect the Christian way of life. They are watching to see what I will do. In their pain and suffering, I see the face of Jesus Christ. They love this place and they have nowhere else to go. I know that God has placed me here so that they will know God's love. My favorite Bible passage is from Romans 8: 'We know that all things work together for good for those who love God, who are called according to God's purposes.' In society we build all sorts of walls that separate people from one another, but I know God loves all humankind. God does not want us to be divided. The church is here so that God's love will be made known to all of us. Love is all about breaking down the barriers that divide. I want to stay here so that we can learn to love each other. I want the people who live here to know that they are loved by God, that they may be comforted."

I was blessed to be able to be there with our partners at a time of severe crisis. I became a living sign of the ties that bind us through the ages. I was also able to serve to connect the international church with the church in Japan as we struggled to bring relief to the suffering. Mission is all about relationships and being present with each other when it counts. God works through these relationships to enable us to be the church and to serve society.

QUESTIONS FOR STUDY AND DIALOGUE:

1. The first story speaks to the need of avoiding "quick fixes" in our mission work. What do you think are examples of "quick fixes" in mission that have either had good results or have had negative short- or long-term consequences?

2. These reflections suggest that our mission is to renew right relationships with God, self, others, and nature. In what ways do you feel that you or your church is taking part in this mission of healing and restoration?

RELATIONSHIPS | **45**

3. The second story speaks of servanthood. What image does your church project in the community in terms of displaying a spirit of Christian service?

4. How should churches handle disagreement about a Christian response to controversial political and social issues? What does it mean to have an international prophetic witness as part of the mission of your church?

5. The third story speaks of helping by recognizing one's own call to help as part of a relationship. Can you think of a time when you have benefited more from giving than the recipient did from receiving?

III | SHARING THE STORY

5

MISSION AND INTERRELIGIOUS DIALOGUE

The Case of Christians and Muslims in the Middle East

Mohammad Sammak

WHAT MAKES A CHRISTIAN in the Middle East wake up and no longer feel safe or accepted—that the only viable option is to pack up and emigrate? The idea of a better life, socially and economically, as well as the increased uncertainty associated with the rise of religious fundamentalism, beliefs that claim to monopolize truth and use violence to terrorize others who are different, are widely cited factors for Christian emigration from the Middle East. Similarly, what makes a Muslim in North America or Europe wake up and no longer identify as a North American or European? What motivates one to become an "Islamic soldier" fighting in a "holy war against the infidel"? Here again, the lure of "jihadism," combined with the feeling of no longer belonging to a place of residence or citizenship, are commonly identified factors.

In a time of heightened sectarianism, not just in the Middle East but indeed worldwide, the importance of proactive and sustained inter-religious engagement is urgent. There are plenty of recent examples of religiously motivated violence—both rhetorical and physical—against people and groups. In Europe, there have been multiple incidents of anti-Semitism, such as a fatal shooting in a Copenhagen synagogue and the

49

50 | SHARING THE STORY

attack on a Jewish-owned market in Paris. Twenty Coptic Christians were beheaded in Libya, and thousands of Christians have been threatened with death or expulsion in Iraq and Syria. Three Muslims were killed in North Carolina, and a Florida pastor declared "International Burn the Qur'an Day" a few years ago. These are just a few of the tragic and abhorrent results of intolerance, negative stereotyping and hatred based on religious identity. Many more examples could be cited around the world, and the media prey on such news. However, there are also committed and faithful people in as many places working vigorously to build up community, interreligious understanding, acceptance, and peace, to change the narrative, and to create healthy community through joint programs. Christians might understand such efforts in terms of mission—a response to God's call to embrace people of their own faith as well as other faiths, relating as sisters and brothers, all of whom are created in God's image. But this calling is not just for Christians. Such a calling is felt among people of many different faiths and is actively and broadly practiced, even if it is not popular fodder for news. Islam also defines a clear and positive relationship with people of other faiths, particularly Christians, and commends its faithful to uphold that relationship in meaningful and necessary ways, as we will see.

The experience of Christians and Muslims in the Middle East, to where both faiths trace their roots but where neither community today finds the majority of its adherents, can be especially informative in exploring the motivations for interreligious dialogue and relations, as well as gleaning some essential principles and guidelines applicable to many different contexts.

CURRENT CONTEXT IN THE MIDDLE EAST

The "Arab Spring" has marked a turning point in the region's history and the consequent changes are witnessed in different ways in Tunisia, Libya, Egypt, Syria, Yemen, Bahrain, and elsewhere. Some transitions have been smooth, while others are ongoing and violent. The outcomes are far from

MISSION AND INTERRELIGIOUS DIALOGUE | 51

certain, but discourse over what makes a democratic liberal country has shifted. Where are the Christians of the Middle East with respect to this change? What role they are playing and what will be the impact of these changes on their presence, role, and future in this region's societies? Will they gain or lose and how will they adjust?

Various authoritarian Arab regimes have used the threat of radical Islam as a scarecrow to maintain their rule and present themselves as acceptable to Western countries. "It's either us or the Islamists" has been their refrain. It has been a convenient arrangement for both the Western states and these regimes, as long as the interests of both are served. The discourse of democracy and human rights has been merely rhetorical, with little bearing on actual policy. Christians of the Middle East were caught in between but were not the only ones to suffer.

A report by the Pew Research Center found that nearly 77 percent of the world's people live in countries with "high restrictions" on religion. After studying 198 countries and self-ruling territories, Pew found that 63 percent have restrictions by local or national authorities ranging from registration requirements to discriminatory policies and outright bans on certain faiths. In 159 countries, faiths are required to register with government, and in 88 states this obligation has caused problems for some religions.[1] The Middle East is not exceptional—there are limits on religious rights here, too. Christians and Muslims suffer the same political, social, and economic hardships, but with the rise of religious fundamentalism—which monopolizes belief and even God—and the fatal mistake of understanding Christianity and the West as synonymous, it is thus not surprising that Christians and Muslims of the Middle East worry about their future.

The broad community of Muslims shares the responsibility of this negative and destructive new development; it is in their national and religious interests to work to put an end to it. First, they must admit that there is a problem, that they are associated with it, and consequently that they have to be part of the solution. Additionally, they have to realize that the more Christians fear and worry about Islamic extremism, the more they will be motivated to emigrate, resulting in an unrecoverable loss of a historic and valued part of Middle Eastern society; a greater proliferation of Islamic extremism in the region and, consequentially, a setback to liberalism, tolerance, and moderation; and a concurrent rise in Islamophobia in the West due to the errant perception that most Muslims are not tolerant or respectful of other religions. Muslim citizens must reconsider their national constitutions to guarantee the rights of equal citizenship to all citizens regardless of their religion or ethnicity, respect freedom of religion, and realize that by doing so they respect their own religion too.

Father Khalil Alwan, the General Secretary of the Eastern Catholic Patriarchs Council, says, "What distinguishes the churches of the East is that they are apostolic, which means that they were established by the apostles: Mark in Egypt and Peter in Lebanon and Syria. We are proud to be Eastern Christians and not Christians in the East. We are of the essence of these countries and part of their formation and history. We are the builders of the Arab civilization and have contributed to the revival of language and culture. Christianity in this East is a rich fortune." Can Islam as a religion co-exist with Christianity? Does it accept and respect Christianity as a religion? And does it recognize the rights of Christians as Christians?

THE ISLAMIC TIE AND OBLIGATION TOWARD CHRISTIANITY

Islam holds that Christianity is a message from God. Jesus Christ is described as the word of God and a spirit from God. Islam says too that God assisted Jesus with the Holy Spirit, revealed to him the Bible, and made him and his followers blessed. The Qur'an says that Jesus, by the will of God, created birds out of clay, healed the sick, and raised the dead. Islam believes in the virginity of Mary, the mother of Jesus Christ, and believes that she was the most chosen and most preferable to God among all women.

The Qur'an says that "there is light and guidance in the Bible" and calls upon Christians to follow what God revealed to them in the Bible.

MISSION AND INTERRELIGIOUS DIALOGUE | 53

The same is said about Judaism and the Torah. According to Islam, the "people of the book," that is, Christians and Jews, are believers in the same God; both the Bible and the Torah are revelations from God; Christianity and Judaism are part of the Islamic tradition; and "harming a Christian in particular is like harming myself," as the prophet Muhammad said.

In general, Islamic ethics and teachings are derived from two sets of principles. First, the Qur'an says that all people and all nations are created from one soul; that, by the will of God, peoples are different and they will remain different until the end of time; and that God requires them to come to know each other and to cooperate for their common good. Second, the Qur'an says that God bestowed dignity on all human beings, regardless of their belief or nonbelief, and regardless of their ethnicity, color, confession, or language. The Prophet was once asked, "Who is the Muslim?" He replied, "The Muslim is he who makes safe all peoples from both his hand and his tongue." That is to say, the one who does no harm to anybody by action (his hand) or even by a word (his tongue) is a true Muslim. The episode is reminiscent of the parable of the good Samaritan, in which a lawyer asked Jesus what he must do to enter the kingdom of heaven. When Jesus told him to "love thy neighbor as yourself," he asked, "And who is my neighbor?"

Christianity occupies an esteemed and prominent status in Islam as a message from God. The prophet Muhammad emphasized this in many of his sayings and actions. For example, the Prophet entered into covenant with the Christians of the Yemeni tribe, the Najran. The covenant states: "That I protect and defend them"—i.e., Christians—"and their churches, houses of worship, monasteries, and pilgrimage sites, wherever they be— in a mountain, a valley, a cave, an urban location, a plain, or a desert." It goes on to promise: "That I safeguard their religion and sect wherever they are—on land or at sea, east or west, the same as I would safeguard myself and my own, and the people of Islam of my own nation." Article 5 of the Najran covenant reads: "No bishop will be removed from his episcopal see, nor any monk from his monastery, and no pilgrim from his pil-

54 | SHARING THE STORY

grimage; none of their churches shall be destroyed, and nothing of their buildings shall be used in the construction of mosques or the houses of Muslims. Whoever does this violates the covenant of God, breaks with God's Prophet, and has removed himself from the protection of God." Article 6 confirms that "No monks and bishops, or those of them that devote themselves to God, or wear wool, or become hermits in the mountains and in remote, isolated places are to be subjected to personal or property tax." It concludes, "No Christian is to be compelled to become a Muslim. 'Do not dispute with the People of the Book except in the better way.' Mercy is to be extended to them and harm is to be kept away from them, wherever they are in the land."[2]

In Saint Catherine's monastery, in the Egyptian Sinai, there is a document signed by the Prophet himself addressed to the Christians. It says, "So whenever a monk or a pilgrim is on a mountain or in a valley, cave, village, plain, church, or temple—we are behind them and they are under our protection. I will fight for them myself and my assistants and followers and for their possessions and temples, for they are my people and my responsibility, so that nobody shall rob their pilgrims or demolish a church of theirs, and nothing of it shall enter a house of any Muslim. Anybody who takes any of it will have broken God's undertaking and contradicted his messenger [Muhammad]. And no taxes shall be levied on their judges, monks, or any of them whose occupation is worship, and no other financial burdens or penalties. For I maintain their protection on land, at sea, in the East, West, North, South, or wherever they are, for they are my responsibility and in the safety of my protection against all that is undesirable to them." The document goes on to say, "And nobody of the Islamic nation shall break this obligation until the Day of Judgment and the end of the world."[3]

The tie of heritage and the commitment to respect Christian presence are therefore embedded in Islamic texts and history. That is why the challenge of religious extremism that Christians in the Middle East face today contradicts the Qur'an and the teachings of prophet Muhammad.

MISSION AND INTERRELIGIOUS DIALOGUE | 55

A CONTEMPORARY COVENANT

Recognizing and believing the indispensable nature of these commitments, and drawing upon a rich history of Christian-Muslim dialogue and social intercourse for more than fourteen centuries in the Middle East, the Arab Group for Muslim-Christian Dialogue was formed in 1995. It has since worked on a host of issues facing our nations and societies throughout the Middle East, such as citizenship, democracy, human rights, coexistence and religious tensions, the place of Jerusalem in our respective traditions, and our common Abrahamic heritage. This group consists of religious, intellectual, and civil society leaders from Lebanon, Syria, Egypt, Palestine, and the Arab Gulf, among other countries in the region, all of whom recognize a faith in the same God and a sense of national belonging. In December 2001, the Arab Group adopted the covenant called "Dialogue and Coexistence: An Arab Muslim-Christian Covenant." The Covenant's significance is in the common recognition of issues faced by Middle Easterners, be they Christian or Muslim, and the commitment to work together to address them. It is built upon personal convictions and is "not simply a dialogue between compatriots [but is] a dialogue among believers who perceive . . . an applied expression of their religious principles, principles that give substance to the meaning of pluralism, mutual recognition, the unqualified dignity of the human being, and the values of justice, fairness, truth, decency, fellow feeling, mercy, and the stewardship of creation."[4]

The members of the Arab Group committed to "strengthening and sustaining dialogue" and undertaking a "practical program aimed at giving firm foundation to coexistence and treating the root causes of confessional religious unrest," which is accounted for by "political, economic, social, and cultural circumstances." It goes on to say that dialogue is a "way of resolving the confusion between genuine religiosity and the objectionable extremism that leads to violence and fanaticism" in order to "foster coexistence." Furthermore, "dialogue is disciplined toward gaining comprehension, mutual understanding, always listening to one another and speaking frankly. It eschews inflammatory and wounding speech. . . . [It] is also a tool for building confidence, for nurturing genuine relationships, and for cultivating friendship."

As a committee comprised of people of faith, the Arab Group "believes that religion cannot be banished from public life; its constructive role therein cannot be denigrated." The covenant concludes by urging "Muslim and Christian religious scholars, people of culture, and intellectuals to look for the spiritual and humanitarian values held in common in the heritage of both religions and in the life styles [sic] of their adherents, as well as for those positive and glowing examples of coexistence, solidarity, compassion, mutual affection, and hold them up to highlight dialogue and tolerance as it is practiced in society as a whole."[5]

These principles and motivations, while agreed upon by our group of Muslim and Christian Middle Easterners, are applicable in most any setting, among adherents of any faith community seeking to engage other communities of faith, working in their societies to break down barriers and build up society. While they may seem self-evident in some ways, they also need to be articulated so that they can come to life and be recognized. And of course, it is not just the agreement of principles, but the process of getting to know one another and building relationships that is especially meaningful.

In the Middle East, as in the United States and elsewhere, the steps to productive dialogue and joint action are similar. The handbook *Living Faithfully in the United States Today* helpfully outlines a process that can be useful. First, a deliberate effort to get to know one another is imperative. Communities may think they know each other through study, through (mis)conceptions, or through personal experience, but there is always more to learn and preconceptions that require adjustment or correction. Second, understanding the issues that are important to each community can be informative and helps to identify issues of common concern. It is possible, and indeed likely, that such a conversation will unearth fears, prejudices, disagreements, and misunderstandings. And ulti-

MISSION AND INTERRELIGIOUS DIALOGUE | 57

mately communities may come to commit to continue to engage and to work together toward "building mutually supporting communities in a pluralistic society."[6]

As Muslims and Christians in the Middle East, we now have the chance to rebuild our societies on the principles of a civil state, equal citizenship, democracy, human rights, and religious freedom. We know that this will not be easy. But we know, too, that Muslims and Christians have to do it together or it will not be done. In the case of the Middle East, our challenges may be under special scrutiny globally. And two of our main religious communities, Islam and Christianity, are presented in ways that are rarely accurate or complete and often unhelpful in the efforts to improve our common future. The attention increases the pressure on us, but also motivates us to make sure that we are remembered for living our faith authentically, according to God's call. The first step in this thousand-mile journey is believing we share a common destiny. If we do, then we must also share in a sense of responsibility and duty. This will determine whether or not we will be together, as sisters and brothers in community.

QUESTIONS FOR STUDY AND DIALOGUE

1. How do you and your church currently relate to people of other faith traditions?

2. This chapter outlines a number of Islamic beliefs and commitments toward Christians. Did any of these beliefs surprise you? How can learning more about the beliefs, practices, and faith of others lead to deeper dialogue?

3. In what ways can you make a deliberate effort to build relationships with people of other faiths locally? Globally?

4. What important issues of common concern can you name locally or globally that could lead to fruitful dialogue and working together with people of other faiths?

DIFFERENT PATHS TO THE DIVINE
BRUCE VAN VOORHIS

Interfaith Cooperation Forum (ICF) is a network in Asia of currently ninety-eight young people in their twenties working in their communities in sixteen countries to address a variety of social, economic, and political issues—the problems faced by women and children, human rights violations, the needs of internally displaced people, the transformation of conflicts, and similar issues.

The premise on which the work of ICF is based is that Asia's major faiths—Buddhism, Christianity, Hinduism, and Islam, as well as the spirituality of the region's indigenous people—share the same core values of respecting all forms of life, acting with compassion, and promoting justice and peace. It is felt that this common bedrock should be a starting point for working together as people of diverse faiths to tackle Asia's significant problems. Moreover, through this cooperative process, relationships can be built over a period of time between people from different faith communities so that "the other" is no longer a Christian or a Muslim, for instance, but is a colleague, a neighbor, a friend—in short, another human being.

Several years ago during ICF's main program, the fourteen-week School of Peace in Bangalore, India, a Jesuit priest with a doctorate in Indian philosophies spoke to the participants about Hinduism. Regarding interfaith relations, he explained that Hindus perceive the Divine Spirit as being at the top of a mountain. Hindus, he said, approach the Divine Spirit from one side of the mountain, Buddhists from another side, Muslims from yet a third side, and Christians from the fourth side of the peak. Viewed this way, all four major faiths relate to the same Divine Spirit, with each approaching the Divine in different ways through different narratives, different teachings, different doctrines, and different rituals.

Adopting this perspective is a way for people of all faiths throughout the world to perhaps live together more peacefully today—a web of relationships our divided and broken world should welcome.

6

EVANGELISM

Reconciling with God, Reconciling with Others

Balázs Ódor, Shin Seung-Min, Elida Quevedo;
Derek Duncan, *editor*

WHEN ONE THINKS about God's mission in the world, evangelism, or sharing God's good news, is central to this task. But how, in a world of different cultures and languages, is evangelism understood and practiced? Are all ways of sharing the good news equally relevant or appropriate? In this chapter, individuals representing partners on three different continents and in three different contexts share how they understand God's call to evangelize, helping us to understand that while God's call is universal, the ways in which we live it out must address the particularities of our society, culture, and historical moment to be meaningful. The three contributors to this chapter are leaders in partner churches of Global Ministries. Each brings a lens through which to understand questions concerning evangelism, and each can, in turn, help us better understand our own calling to share God's good news.

CALLED TO BE AMBASSADORS FOR CHRIST
Balázs Ódor

When I reflect on concepts and practices of evangelism with a special focus on the post-Soviet or post-Communist context, I have to start with a clarification. It would be inaccurate to suggest there is one clear concept of evangelism that would be applicable to Eastern European Protestant churches. The way we understand and practice mission and evangelism differs even within my own church, the Reformed Church in Hungary (RCH), and it differs within the larger Hungarian Reformed community found in several countries of Eastern Europe. Although we speak the same language, share the same history, and have a common theological and confessional background, we have differing convictions, passions, and practices.

This applies to the whole region of Europe formerly under Soviet rule. There are countries that figure among the most secular regions of Europe, such as the Czech Republic or the former East Germany; others, such as Poland, would make us believe that after the political changes at the beginning of the 1990s, religion spontaneously started to flourish. From a sociological point of view there is no apparent trend within the groups of Eastern and Western countries. Secularization, individualization, and privatization are prevalent, but none of these dynamics alone can universally explain religious trends in Europe.

Consequently, I would argue there is no unique and typical way that God's people in post-Communist countries would think and act and live out their calling. This assessment might seem discouraging and disappointing when one tries to grasp and classify the "special flavor" of fellow Christians' approach and life in a different context. It is, however, a necessary clarification. Nevertheless, I will share my personal impressions and stories in a way that may help readers see what is particular to us.

In every family, stories that capture important moments in life are told to the children. In my family's case, one of these edifying stories was about my grandmother. She was a "normal," faithful member of the Re-

formed community, a model of a kind but strict and puritan woman,
nonetheless stopped going to church and joined the ruling party in the
1960s because she wanted to become director of the school where she
worked as a teacher. The strategy proved to be successful. But this moment, captured in the family saga, represented a shameful denial of faith.

Under the Communist rule, churches and religion were persecuted
and Christians intimidated by deportation or imprisonment. Most people
were under similar pressure as my grandmother. Church life was allowed,
but only "within the walls." All institutions, like schools, traditionally established to reach out to society—all organized means of social ministries—were confiscated and mission activities forbidden. The ruling party
was convinced that religion would disappear from society. It did not.

At the end of the day, when the Communist regime collapsed, the
Hungarian church was confronted with a situation that I would describe
as sort of a double impact of secularizing tendencies. We lost, in a way, a
whole generation, that of my parents, whose majority never had a "natural" relationship with the church. On the other hand, we were faced with
similar, if not identical, developments as Western European countries.
There was a brief period that we experienced as a religious revival. The
number of students with different social and family backgrounds increased
suddenly at the seminaries in the early 1990s, for example. Thus, we have
a lot of young pastors and conferences where the average age is around
thirty-five. It would be easy, however, to overestimate this temporary social
phenomenon. Similarly, it would also be wrong to assume that the operation of reclaimed educational and social institutions, which were returned
to the church after the regime change, would make reorientation and renewal in mission unnecessary.

In the last twenty-five years, we have been struggling for a renewed
identity in a new, rapidly changing context. Switching from "survival
mode" to "free operation" has been a real challenge. Sorting out what we
can learn from the past and where we should find orientation for the future takes much more time than some could have ever foreseen. We are

still in this learning process. Some, though fewer and fewer, still complain about what we have lost in the past and wish that everything could be restored as it used to be. Others, growing in number and in awareness, are developing a future-oriented perspective of God's coming realm and trust that fresh ways of mission and evangelism will fuel our communities in seasons and years to come. This means revealing the way of a church whose congregations "shall proclaim the life-shaping message of the Gospel to marginalized groups, including the large Roma population"— as it reads in the recently adopted Roma Strategy of the RCH.[1]

This implies a paradigm shift in understanding evangelism. Too often evangelization in the RCH still addresses those who are already members of the congregations, whose aims are the renewal and revitalization of their own faith. But more and more, our community seeks fresh ways of evangelizing, of reaching out to society and going beyond the walls of the church. In the commitment to a renewed, mission-oriented life of the church, we come very close to an understanding of the Christian community and discipleship that finds its expression in so many reflections, prayers, and theological documents of world Christianity. As the renewed vision of the RCH, formulated recently by a church revision committee, expresses it, "The community of the Church is called to be a sign, foretaste and servant of the kingdom of God in the world through its congregations and church members, who proclaim the Gospel of Christ to the world both with words and deeds."[2]

This growing missionary awareness is reflected also in the motto of the RCH: "Ambassadors for Christ." This expression, from 2 Corinthians 5:20, points to reconciliation in Christ as a "gift and task" of which the church in its very being is called to be a sign and agent. Paul's image reflects the inseparable character of the church as living communion and as an agent of mission in the world. We were pardoned. We have been liberated. We have been reconciled. Our lives have changed once and for all. We are enabled thus to take on the office of reconciliation, just as Paul did even in difficult times. God has reconciled us in Christ. The "Still-

EVANGELISM | 63

Speaking God" calls this into our mind powerfully so that we do not rely on our human approach and perspective anymore, but represent somehow the way God regards us in Christ. This is the basis of evangelism.

A statement of the World Council of Churches Commission on World Mission and Evangelism, "Together towards Life: Mission and Evangelism in Changing Landscapes," states, "As the church discovers more deeply its identity as a missionary community, its outward-looking character finds expression in evangelism."[3] This formulation describes the transition the RCH is making in these days. In this way, we can share the passion for mission with Christian communities around the world as we share more and more the same vision and language in and beyond various contexts and traditions.

AN INCLUSIVE UNDERSTANDING OF MISSION
Shin Seung-Min

Let me begin my reflection with a story of a long-term political prisoner, Choi In-Jung. He was born in North Korea in 1927. He completed his higher education in North Korea, became a Labor Party member, and worked with the government transportation department. He got married and had four children. They made a happy family until he was dispatched to South Korea as a spy in 1964. Just two days after his arrival in the South, he was arrested by the police and charged with espionage. He served twenty-three years in prison and was released in 1988. But in 1990, just two years after his release, he was diagnosed as being in the last stages of liver cancer. He struggled with the cancer for almost a year and died on November 21, 1991. Just a few months before his death, he wrote an open letter to his wife in North Korea saying that "my only wish before I die is to see you and our children and say sorry to them about all [that] happened to us."

On October 1991, just a month before his death, Choi sent his open letter to the Human Rights department of the National Council of Churches in Korea (NCCK), with which I worked as an executive secretary.

His letter was full of deep feelings of suffering and sorrow, representing the tragic situation of division in Korea. My department immediately contacted the Unification Ministry of the South Korean government to request a short meeting between Choi and his family. Fortunately, the Unification Ministry accepted our request and asked us to send an application form by November 20. The meeting was scheduled for twenty to thirty minutes on December 31 in the Joint Security Area of Panmunjom. I contacted Choi, and he was very excited and happy about the news and agreed to travel from his place to Seoul on November 20 to submit the application form. But unfortunately he could not make it because of his worsening sickness. On the following day, November 21, he died, longing for his family in North Korea. After his death we appealed to the South Korean government to hand over his letter to his wife, but the government refused, being afraid of facing thousands of similar requests from the separated families in South Korea. We were eventually able to deliver his letter to his wife with the help of the World Council of Churches (WCC). This is one of many tragic stories heard in the Korean peninsula since its division in 1953.

The division had already started with Korea's liberation in 1945, when the Soviet Union took control of the northern part of Korea and the United States occupied the southern part of the peninsula. As a result of the Korean War from 1950 to 1953, three years in which more than six million people were killed and the entire country was completely destroyed, the division became an unavoidable reality. More than sixty years of division has caused confrontation and antagonism between two Koreas, bringing unbearable *han*, a mixture of sorrow and resentment, to the *minjung*, or grassroots people. There are still more than one hundred twenty thousand separated families in South Korea and their number is increasing as *saetemin*, or defectors from North Korea, are gradually on the rise.

Since the division, the capitalist South and the socialist North have constantly created a fear in the differences between each other, while reinforcing among their people an acceptance of uniformity, claiming difference and otherness as serious threats. This fear was used, especially by military regimes in the South, as an excuse to oppress and dominate. Even the church in Korea has reinforced the fear, offering "safe havens from difference, welcoming only certain groups, and misusing theological teachings to exclude those who don't fit."[4]

The story of the Tower of Babel (Gen. 9:1–11) tells us about God's rejection of the tower builders' attempt to force uniformity by controlling different groups of people with a single language, culture, or political structure. God descended, confused the languages of the people, and scattered them all over the earth, condemning the tower builders' universalizing project. In this story, God reaffirms the beauty of diversity bestowed in creation. The Tower of Babel shows us that difference (diversity) is not a punishment by God, but a gift of God.

For the last two decades, direct encounters, exchanges, and various joint events between North and South Korean churches have dramatically increased. In the midst of the struggle to embrace the differences, the churches began to realize that their difference is not a punishment, but God's precious blessing. They also realized that renouncing forced uniformity and embracing difference is a wonderful gift from the postcolonializing God, who proclaims that difference can be a power on behalf of emancipation rather than being a structural weapon used for domination.

God's shalom is not possible without a true reconciliation with our sisters and brothers around the world. Matthew 5:23–24 (NIV) says, "if you are offering your gift at the altar and there remember that your brother or sister has something against you . . . first go and be reconciled to them; then come and offer your gift." Reconciliation with people is a prerequisite to reconciliation with God and to the long process of true repentance, justice, forgiveness, and healing. The liberating God calls us today to participate in a mission of reconciliation, which embraces otherness, renounces hegemony, and, in a spirit of pluralism, respects the values of others. For all of us, this mission is not an option; reconciliation is an urgent need as we live among all forms of violence caused by reinforced uniformity and domination.

ELEMENTS FOR LIBERATING EVANGELIZATION
Elida Quevedo

During the conquest of Latin America, Christian evangelization was accomplished by blood and fire, leading to the geographical invasion and genocide of indigenous peoples and civilizations in these lands. Beginning in the fifteenth century, primarily Spanish and Portuguese explorers and missionaries sought to propagate the Christian faith using the power of arms and political coercion, having little to no respect for the indigenous cultures, beliefs, and practices they encountered.

While Christian evangelization by blood and fire is a method of the past, even the current ways, although more attractive and seductive, are not always relevant to the social and cultural realities experienced in the world today.

Biblically, to evangelize means to fill the world with the good news of God. This gospel must extend to all corners of the earth, contribute to the integrity of the person and the whole of creation, and lead to transformation and liberation by the working of the Holy Spirit and the Word of God. As such, a relevant evangelization is one that can influence the transformation of negative realities—realities of suffering—and turn them into new realities of hope for humanity and for the creation of God. Unfortunately, some models of evangelization are limited to only one of the foundational understandings of the gospel, rejecting this comprehensive and liberating perspective.

In Venezuelan Pentecostalism, there are various experiences of evangelism. I will present three of the most representative, including the experience of the Evangelical Pentecostal Union of Venezuela (UEVP).[5]

One understanding of evangelization drives the prosperity gospel movements. This type of evangelism greatly uses communications media, centered in the act of proclamation and undertaken through large gatherings where a preacher employs the work of conviction. The message is aimed at those hoping to receive miracles in their lives and focuses on making covenants with God through contributions of money or material things, by which the petitioner expects to receive some benefit in return. The attribute of Jesus that stands out in the prosperity message is the power to do miracles. People seek from the gospel the power to remove from their lives diseases or impediments to success, both economic success and prosperity in general terms, and they are willing to pay for it.

Another model of evangelization prevalent in Venezuelan churches is the neo-Pentecostal orientation,[6] which maintains an emphasis on evangelization aimed primarily at attracting people to their religious movement. The message is central with a strong spiritual content, but offers few details regarding the person and life of Jesus of Nazareth and very little that promotes an ethic of Christian responsibility for the world. The whole aim of religious education is oriented towards the singular goal of proclamation in order to proselytize.

This reductionism of evangelical foundations is contradictory to biblical perspectives that go far beyond the mere proclamation of the message of the risen Jesus. Much more than simple belief is necessary in order for people to follow him. This is the direction given in Mark 16:15 (NIV): "Go into all the world and preach the gospel." There are also the lessons of Matthew 28:18–20 ("Go and make disciples of all nations") and Luke 24:48 ("You are witnesses of these things"), which also point towards teaching, obedience, and testimony as fundamental principles. According to these texts, to evangelize implies believing, proclaiming, witnessing, and learning to live personally and socially all that Jesus has commanded us. From this brief background, we can get a third example of evangelism by looking at the understanding and practice of the UEPV.

The movement UEPV inherited from its originator, Pastor Frederick Bender Geother, is a theological understanding of evangelization as service to communities in need, such as orphaned boys and girls, which was later expanded to include peasant struggles, indigenous populations, and women—all of whose experiences gradually contributed to the under-

68 | **SHARING THE STORY**

standing of evangelism through service. Most comprehensively, evangelism in the UEPV contains the following liberating characteristics: it is (1) preferential to the poor, (2) ecumenical, (3) inclusive, (4) ecological, (5) liturgical, and (6) opposed to all discrimination.

The preferential option for the poor is paramount. This is grounded in Luke 4:18 (with reference to Isaiah 61:1–2a, and Isaiah 35), in which Jesus claims the prophetic mandate "to bring good news to the poor . . . release to the captives and recovery of sight to the blind, to let the oppressed go free. . . ." Luke presents evangelization as the pronouncement of God's good news of salvation and liberation aimed at those who are oppressed and in need. Jesus is the messenger of God, so long awaited, who finally arrives at a particular historical time to fulfill these promises of deliverance to a suffering and desperate people. The same content appeared when John wanted to know if Jesus was indeed the one for whom they were waiting (Mark 11:1–6). Jesus responded with how he understood his calling, as we see, for example, in Luke 4:18.

An ecumenical calling conveys the good news of transformation to a world divided by religious, racial, gender, cultural, political, and other distinctions—a world threatened on all sides by senseless wars. Since its inception, the UEPV assumed an evangelical approach that was ecumenical in character. In 1961 it signed an Agreement of Unity and Mutual Cooperation with the Christian Church (Disciples of Christ) in the United States and Canada, and later extended to the United Church of Christ in the United States. In 1987, this ecumenical commitment was publicly ratified, the basics of which are laid out in the Charter of Valencia.[7]

A commitment to inclusivity is also an element of the gospel because it strengthens the creative capacities of individuals, leading them to transformation and liberation by the working of the Holy Spirit and the Word of God. In January 2007, the UEPV adopted a democratic and participatory structure that is now the key to the development of its ministries. It has Regional Development Pastoral Councils and specific pastoral guidelines at local, regional, and national levels, which have the autonomy to carry out tasks concerning their basic functions. This structure allows power to be shared in ways that uplift those who, in the past, have been marginalized.

An ecological evangelism addresses the crises affecting the planet in order to ensure human survival and the salvation of nature in its entirety. All evangelical activity is accompanied by a liturgical component that affirms life and hope, incorporating the beauty of art in prayer. Evangelism that struggles against all discrimination requires us to address problems of gender, racism, absolutism, fundamentalism, and all such forms of oppression. An example of this experience of evangelism in the UEPV is the current program "Black and Indigenous Pastors against All Discrimination," which began in 1986. At that time it was focused on the indigenous sector of the Wayuu ethnic group that was part of the UEPV. This community had been part of the UEPV for seventy years, but went unnoticed in the organizational structure of the church.

The challenge then was, through critical, intercultural, and interreligious dialogue, to persuade the organization of churches to intentionally strengthen this area in order to eradicate racial discrimination and *endorracismo*, or internalized racism. The process helped restore this community's own cultural values, creating spaces for social and ecclesial participation and ensuring their human and social development through community health days, intercultural encounters, and other activities of solidarity.

After twenty-eight years of spreading this good news, there is significant progress in the quality of life for the Wayuu community. The emphasis on inclusivity has allowed Wayuu leaders to take charge of their own process of raising self-awareness and transformation. Currently, their involvement in the life and organization of the UEPV is very visible and significant, now spreading the gospel both in the church as well as in their own communities, to further advance an antiracist consciousness and opposition to all discrimination.

I conclude this reflection with an appeal to the responsibility we have as Christians to bring the magnificent good news of God, a message of liberation and transformation, wherever it is needed. For the church and its people this is a call to mission. While we all agree that evangelism is necessary, the question before us is "are we called to an evangelism of service?"

Our world is in crisis. When we share the gospel, how aware are we of the realities of suffering and oppression that need the good news of God today? The answer to this question may determine what "the Lord requires" of us and where we are called to serve. The challenge might seem huge, but would we surrender without trying?

May God's Holy Spirit enable us to persevere and God's Word guide us in this time. As we seek to share the gospel of Christ to a world of suffering and groaning (Rom. 8:18–23), may our message bring hope for a future of abundant life and peace.

QUESTIONS FOR STUDY AND DIALOGUE

1. The first perspective on evangelism speaks of the Christian community in post-Soviet Europe moving from a mode of "survival" to "free operation." How do we as individuals and as faith communities value the experience, in some cases, of merely keeping the faint light of faith alive during dark times, even as we explore ways to apply the renewal of our faith into ministry "beyond the walls of the church"?

2. Does "developing a future-oriented perspective of God's coming realm" and exploring "fresh ways of evangelizing, of reaching out to society" rely first on focusing on our inward needs as Christians for revival and transformation—in order to "represent somehow the way God regards us in Christ"? Are there ways we are transformed inwardly through our ministry and engagement with others beyond the walls of the church?

3. The account of the Korean church's reunification ministry emphasizes that healing and reconciliation of society as a whole, what many call social justice, is an aspect of evangelism. How can demonstrating God's promise of reconciliation and acceptance in the world draw people to the church? Does your church make an explicit connection between its church growth ministries and its social justice ministries?

EVANGELISM | 71

4. How is an understanding of God as one who "reaffirms the beauty of diversity in creation" related to an evangelical commitment to ensure that differences in the human community are not used to discriminate or exert power or privilege over others?

5. In the third reflection, the author says "a relevant evangelization is one that can influence the transformation of negative realities—realities of suffering—and turn them into new realities of hope for humanity and for the creation of God." For the church in Venezuela, making God's good news relevant for the indigenous Wayuu meant transforming oppressive social systems on the outside as well as healing internalized racism on the inside. How do we discern God's call to proclaim a good news of "transformation and liberation" that is relevant to our situation?

6. Jesus claimed the prophetic mandate to be an agent of liberation: "to bring good news to the poor . . . release to the captives and recovery of sight to the blind, to let the oppressed go free . . ." (Luke 4:18). As Christian disciples and as the church, what are some concrete ways we can do this?

IV | WORKING FOR
PEACE WITH
JUSTICE

7

CHANGED THROUGH SERVING
Engaging in Advocacy

Peter Shober, Scott Nicholson, Grace Bunker

MANY OF US, when engaged in the vital work of advocacy, both in North America and around the world, work to change both the situations of poverty and injustice in which people live as well as the oppressive systems responsible for these situations. What we may not be aware of, however, is how engagement in advocacy can change us. Below you will find three reflections from people who are all involved with the same partner, the Home of Hope and Peace (HEPAC) in Nogales, Mexico. From their various experiences and perspectives, they share how working for justice not only makes a difference to those with whom we work, but allows God to work in our lives to change us and our view of the world in profound ways.

GOING DEEPER IN MISSION
Peter Shober

Taking mission seriously and advocating on justice issues has never been all that debatable at University UCC in Missoula, Montana. Somewhere, hardwired into our DNA, is the good and gracious notion that we simply must be involved in "the world" if we are to exist as a church that is anywhere close to what a church is called to be. We certainly are not alone with this characterization, but ours really is a church that has created a legacy of being an "activist" congregation. As pastor of this church, I am humbled to look back and recognize what a difference this commitment has made in this church's long history. I am humbled, as well, to see how this has been a grassroots, not top-down, dynamic. I don't pull people along on this mission road; they lead each other, finding new avenues to take and new ways to take them.

Mission, however, takes many forms and few of us would come up with identical definitions of what it is. We have talked about that a good deal here and have come to realize that not one size of mission and advocacy fits all. We also realize that mission today is going to be different than mission was a generation ago. Through a recent long-term vision process, we have been able to discern that we as a congregation, in the midst of this rapidly changing world, are called to "go deeper" in five ways. One of those ways is with what we called "transformational mission." (The other four are going deeper in being a welcoming place for youth and young adults, in becoming a "green" congregation that encourages sustainable lifestyles, in spiritual formation, and in small group ministry.)

The general understanding of "transformational mission" is contrasted with what might be experienced as "transactional mission." We seek not simply to pay for our mission as we might in the marketplace, giving money to someone (or some group) to do something on our behalf, but to engage the whole of ourselves in various mission involvements, so in the process we are changed—changed into people who, from firsthand experience, recognize that servanthood is a foundational element in our commitment to following Jesus. To serve, one must often go to the broken places, which always includes our own brokenness.

One of the avenues we have been given is the creation of a partnership with HEPAC in Nogales, Mexico. HEPAC and folks from Nogales have become our friends—we travel there and they have come to Montana. We tell our stories, we create relationships, and we are informed and changed. Both groups—in differing ways—have been drawn into the issue of immigration and borderlands justice. Why get involved in immigration issues in Montana? We, too, are a border state and we see what is happening in Arizona and recognize some of the same issues here. We are also becoming much more aware of both documented and undocumented workers in our state who often go unseen. We have been able to travel the miles to Nogales and are becoming more able to advocate for border and immigration justice and work with groups here in Montana. When we go to Nogales, we do so involved, to varying degrees, with service projects, immersion experiences, and advocacy. We are deeply impacted by the people we meet and the groups who show us their work on the borders and their tireless efforts to create a more just, safe place for the thousands of profoundly vulnerable people on the border.

It is pivotal to us that our trips are intergenerational; about half of our participants have been teenagers. These trips have been profound for the adults and life-changing for the young folks. Our conviction with this partnership recognizes that we are not going to Nogales to somehow "fix" anything, but rather to be transformed through relationship, witnessing to a profoundly different culture, economy, and political situation, and knowing that our privileged context needs to be seen and put into a broader context.

Indeed, if there were two concepts I would specifically want to lift up as being deeply challenging and invitational with this partnership, it would be how we might deal with issues of privilege and mutuality. How can we, from a university setting in Montana, enter into a mutually respectful relationship when we are the beneficiaries of privilege, which helps to create the very brokenness we seek to witness to and, in the process, become advocates against? One can't help but reflect upon the adage that "the meaning of the gospel is to comfort the afflicted and afflict the comfortable." We are trying to learn how to live out both.

Not everyone desires or is able to go to Nogales and not everyone is drawn to border and immigration justice issues. But there are other arrows in the quiver of mission here, including partnerships and volunteer opportunities with our local homeless shelter, food bank, Family Promise, and Habitat for Humanity. Our hope is that we can help create a congregational culture where mission and advocacy do not exist on the periphery when time and money allow, but are elemental to our identity. We feel the HEPAC partnership is very transformational for those who are involved with it, and we also feel as if we are creating a sustainable model of mission—our expenses are kept quite low and we are able to travel to the U.S./Mexican border without undo complexity. We also endeavor to live out this partnership with other churches in Montana that would like to participate with us. We very much want to keep it simple and do mission partnerships in ways that promote genuine solidarity between people.

LOVING YOUR NEIGHBOR AS YOURSELF
Scott Nicholson

A twenty-five-foot high steel wall separates our neighbors in Nogales, Sonora, from Nogales, Arizona. The border wall was initially built by the Clinton administration in 1994—the same year that the North America Free Trade Agreement (NAFTA) was enacted. NAFTA enabled U.S. corporations to move their capital and products easily across the border in search of higher profits. However, Mexican workers are prohibited from crossing that same border to seek higher wages to support their families.

There are nearly one hundred *maquiladoras* (assembly plants) in Nogales, Sonora, where the minimum wage is $5.20 per day as compared to $8.05 per hour in Nogales, Arizona. The U.S. government recently spent $187 million to modernize the port-of-entry to make it easier for hundreds of trucks to cross daily with products and produce from Sonora. The government also spent tens of millions of dollars to install a taller and stronger wall to prevent unauthorized immigrants from crossing.

"We celebrate unity," said Bill Clinton at the site of the former wall that separated West Berlin from East Berlin in June 1994. "We stand where crude walls of concrete separated mother from child and we meet as one family. We stand where those who sought a new life instead found death. . . . Berliners, you have proved that no wall can forever contain the mighty power of freedom." Four months later, his administration built the Nogales wall.

The border enforcement policy started by Clinton is based on a "prevention through deterrence" strategy. The goal was to "raise the risk . . . to the point that many will consider it futile to attempt illegal entry. . . . Illegal traffic will be deterred or forced over more hostile terrain less suited for crossing."[1]

According to the German government, 138 people were killed while trying to cross the Berlin Wall during the twenty-eight years that it existed. In 2010 alone, 254 migrants lost their lives in the desert of southern Arizona.

George Bush expanded the policy of deterrence during his administration and Barack Obama has escalated it even further. There are now more than five thousand Customs and Border Protection agents stationed along the border in Arizona, and helicopters and drones patrol the skies.

Elbit Systems, a private Israeli military manufacturer, has been contracted to build a "virtual wall" of surveillance towers to the north of the actual border. The towers will include the latest in cameras, radar, and ground sensors; construction started near Nogales in early 2015. Elbit has years of experience with enforcing the borders imposed on the Palestininian people.

When the president and Congress talk about border security they neglect to mention the violent history that created the current boundaries of the United States. The states of California, Arizona, New Mexico, and Texas and parts of Nevada, Utah, Colorado, and Wyoming are located in what used to be northern Mexico. The original inhabitants of the entire Western Hemisphere suffered genocide by the European invasion and occupation of their territory.

80 | WORKING FOR PEACE WITH JUSTICE

"When we hear about more money being spent for 'national security,' we become frightened," says Jeannette Pazos, director of the HEPAC community center in Nogales, Sonora. "The community on this side of the border asks, 'Who are you protecting yourself from?' The wall is a form of structural violence used to keep cheap labor over here."

HEPAC recognizes freedom of movement as a human right but its main focus is on creating a healthy and sustainable community in Mexico so that people aren't forced to risk arrest and death in the desert in a desperate attempt to emigrate to the United States. "We don't want any more mass exodus of people," explains Jeannette. "We want migration to once again be an option rather than a forced decision."

The community programs of HEPAC include lunch for schoolchildren; adult education that enables people to complete elementary and high school; Culture of Peace workshops that provide tools for healing from trauma and violence, and for transforming conflict; and Kids Camps during school vacation that focus on the Culture of Peace.

"We know that the system that created this situation is not capable of fixing it," states Jeannette. "We believe in the power of organized communities to make change and we start by trying to heal our own roots. We're not trying to change the world, we're just trying to remove the pieces of the system that we carry inside us."

Education is a central component and Jeannette often quotes the Brazilian community educator Paolo Freire, who wrote about a system of alternative education that enables communities to generate their own solutions.[2] She says, "Traditional education emphasizes competition. We promote values for life like cooperation, win-win, solidarity, and respect."

Kids Camps take place during school vacation and focus on the Culture of Peace—teaching children about their rights and responsibilities and how to defend their rights. Interacting with puppets, performing mime skits, and creating art enable the participants to express their experiences with violence. The children also work in the garden, which grows vegetables for the lunch program.

"Growing up as a child on the border is like being in a narrow hallway with no options," explains Jeannette. "You may have come from the south of the country and you're not able to return there, or you may have been unwanted and deported from the other side (the United States). We don't want the border to be seen as just a place of violence, misfortune, and deportation. We want the children to realize that this is also sacred ground and a land of opportunity."

Church and school groups from the United States come to HEPAC to learn from the people who are suffering the impact of current economic and immigration policies, and to be inspired by grassroots organizations that are providing humanitarian aid and working to create a more just future. "No matter how tall the wall is there will always be arms that are even longer, so that we can reach across and embrace each other," concludes Jeannette.

BEING LED BY THE SPIRIT AND OUR PARTNERS!
A PERSONAL REFLECTION
Grace Bunker

North American Protestants officially began engaging in international mission with the creation of the American Board of Commissioners for Foreign Missions (ABCFM) in 1810. The first mission station, the Marathi Mission, was established in Bombay, India, in 1813. Over the next 160 years, thousands of men and women of all denominations—generations of my family among them—traveled throughout the world teaching about God's love in Jesus and helping to raise the standard of living for poor and disadvantaged peoples through education, medical care, construction of roads, improvement of agricultural practices, vocational training, child care, advocacy for women, and much more.

The first ABCFM missionaries were my great aunt Helen Richards and her husband, Ephraim Weston Clark, who served in Hawaii. Helen's niece, Belle Richards, married Fred Bunker and they served the ABCFM in southern Africa. Three of their four sons became Congregational ministers and their daughter went into Christian Education. Their son, Sydney, my father, and his wife, Ruth Culbertson, my mother, accepted ABCFM's offer to go as educational missionaries to Jaffna, Ceylon (now Sri Lanka), in 1937. There my sister, Charlotte, and I were born and reared. We attended an American Mission boarding school in Kodaikanal in the hills of South India through high school, spending our long vacations at home in Ceylon. You could say that Christian mission work was bred into us.

Charlotte went to Turkey for three years with the renamed ABCFM, the United Church Board for World Ministries (UCBWM), out of college in 1961, but I resisted all such suggestions. Instead I traveled the globe teaching English. At age fifty-eight, I finally returned to Jaffna, Sri Lanka, as a missionary with Global Ministries. Arriving in the middle of a civil war, I was the only salaried missionary in Jaffna in 2001.

In the years since these early days of North American international mission, the thrust of Christian work has changed enormously. Nearly gone are career missionaries. Most now go for shorter periods of time serving alongside and at the invitation of partners who are nationals. While North Americans who serve do have gifts to share, we also have much to learn from the various ministries of our partners as they seek to be a faithful presence of love and grace in their own context. And in the midst of this giving and receiving, the cross-cultural relationships and trust that built through service together help us realize we are one body.

And that brings me to the mission project that a group of women in Casas Adobes Congregational Church (CACC-UCC) in Tucson, Arizona, started in 2013. When I returned to Tucson after ten years away in Sri Lanka and North Carolina, I found it impossible to ignore the glaring injustices on the Mexican/U.S. border in Nogales, less than a hundred miles south of Tucson.

My involvement began at the Annual Meeting of the Southwest Conference of the UCC (SWC-UCC) in 2012, which was centered on immigrant justice issues. I was deeply moved by Miguel de la Torre's dramatic speech and his book *Reading the Bible from the Margins*. A few months later, I attended the SWC-UCC workshop "Becoming an Immigrant-Welcoming Congregation." I became convinced that, as a people of faith, we needed to engage in this important justice issue. I really focused after attending a conference on border injustices with my friend Toña Morales-Calkins. There, we joined a coalition to end Operation Streamline, a government initiative that rushes immigrants apprehended without papers through the court system in one day instead of the usual process that can take weeks. In addition, immigrants are often treated in rough and disrespectful ways while in detention. Toña and I attended meetings and took part in demonstrations to draw the attention of the public to the unfairness of this program.

I also learned that Global Ministries missionary Scott Nicholson was working in a community center called HEPAC in Nogales, Sonora, Mexico. After I contacted him, Scott met with us to see if we could work together to benefit HEPAC and to educate the members of Casas Adobes Congregational Church. Scott agreed to lead a tour for church members to Nogales to make clear the plight of those who are deported. Frustrated with the slow pace of policy change on immigration, our small group of inspired women began knitting and crocheting for HEPAC's children. We called our group Needlework for Nogales Children (N4NC). Two new members pointed out that we should be working with Mexican women so that they could do their own needlecraft. We met with the director of HEPAC, Jeannette Pazos, to get permission to give lessons to HEPAC volunteers. HEPAC's aim became ours: to provide the skills that would eventually empower local women to increase the family income so no family member would feel a need to make the perilous crossing into the United States through the Sonoran Desert of southern Arizona.

In May 2013, three of us crossed the border and were transported to HEPAC. For two years now Michelle Perrin, Toña, and I, and occasionally others from N4NC, have gone almost every Monday to HEPAC to teach and work with the women. Their skills have increased and we are now able to sell their work in churches, retirement homes, and two stores in Tucson. They also sell their work at HEPAC to the groups who go there to learn about the border situation as described by Scott in the preceding section. Through these two years, communities of women deeply devoted to each other have been created: N4NC women call each other sister-friend, the women at HEPAC are now a close community, and these two groups have become one community of love, admiration, and joy.

We have involved CACC-UCC members by recruiting people to make sweaters and necklaces and to contribute needlework supplies, yarn, and fabric. We collected coats for people living in extreme poverty in a city dump near HEPAC, who earn a living by scavenging and recycling what they find. In eight days, congregants donated more than a hundred coats. They have bought the Nogales women's work. Each winter, Scott leads tours, which many say have changed their lives. Congregants have come to hear a panel of speakers with varying experiences on the border and to hear Rev. John Fife, a leader of the Sanctuary movement in the 1980s, who continues to advocate with great effectiveness for immigrant justice.

In all of this, we have followed HEPAC's lead and supported what they believe is the most important work for them to do. We have always kept front and center in our minds that we are called to walk with this vitally important community center as it becomes better able to raise the standard of living for local people. In this relationship, we have been constantly aware of the leading of the Holy Spirit, and sometimes we have to run to keep up!

QUESTIONS FOR STUDY AND DIALOGUE

1. Given the privileged status of U.S. church groups traveling to less privileged places, is partnership even possible? What questions and conditions need to be addressed?

2. What does it mean to be a learner instead of a teacher when we do mission?

3. What would a "transformative" mission experience look like? What emotions would it spark? What biblical and theological images emerge for you?

8

HOW CAN ADVOCACY HEAL?

Mery Kolimon and Karen Campbell-Nelson

A GRANDMOTHERS' GROUP

It was Paoina's idea: "Let's invite the '1965' grandmothers to gather and pray." Paoina was referring to women in their sixties and seventies who survived the horrifying violence and systematic discrimination that targeted suspected Communists in Indonesia's massive anti-Communist purges of 1965–66. The initial idea was to provide a safe space for the women to support and comfort each other, something still needed decades after the event. Paoina's idea came to fruition with the first gathering in October 2013, and her name for the group, Elderly Prayer Friends, has stuck.

The identity of the participants as survivors of the 1965 Tragedy has determined the group's agenda, which goes beyond bimonthly prayer and Bible study. These grandmothers have encouraged each other to share their stories of abuse, discrimination, and survival in public, a courageous demonstration of words that align with action. Since the group's inception, some members have spoken in public not only locally, but also on a national platform. In December 2013, one grandmother participated in a national event at which survivors of state violence throughout Indonesia shared their ex-

87

periences. Another traveled to Jakarta in April 2014 to participate in the national book launching of *Memori-Memori Terlarang* [*Forbidden Memories*].[1]

Over the months, Elderly Prayer Friends has broadened its activities to include an advocacy agenda that seeks acknowledgement and apology from both church and state for harm done in the past. The truth about the illegal detentions, torture, and killings of 1965–66 has been successfully suppressed in Indonesia for nearly half a century. Elderly Prayer Friends recall how some church members were perpetrators of the 1965 violence and ongoing ostracism. Some of these perpetrators are still alive. In this context, a meeting of 1965 victims and perpetrators to speak and listen to each other could be a valuable contribution towards healing broken trust and relationships. Therefore, Elderly Prayer Friends, along with members of the Eastern Indonesian Women's Network (JPIT), met with the Synod Moderator of their denomination to discuss a process of reconciliation. Another advocacy initiative has been an effort to support the women in seeking to fulfill their social-economic rights. This includes an inventory both of the women's current economic and health conditions and of government services for which they may be eligible.

Through steps like these, Elderly Prayer Friends seeks to integrate spiritual nurturing, attention to social-economic needs, and human rights advocacy—issues often addressed separately.

BURIED HORRORS: 1965

In late 1965, massacres began throughout East Nusa Tenggara (Nusa Tenggara Timur/NTT) Province.[2] The killing of seven generals on September 30, 1965, that was blamed on the Indonesian Communist Party (Partai Komunis Indonesia/PKI) became the excuse for detaining, torturing, and killing those accused as members and sympathizers of the PKI.[3] The army worked with police and youth groups, including church youth groups, to destroy the PKI that was, in fact, a legally recognized party at the time. By sheer number, the PKI was the second largest Communist party in the world.

From 1963 to 1966 a serious drought throughout NTT prompted aid from government, religious, and political organizations. One group providing aid was the Indonesian Farmers' Front (Barisan Tani Indonesia/BTI), an organizational wing of the PKI. Although most people who received this aid had no understanding of the BTI or the PKI, the BTI's lists of aid recipients were later used by the military to arrest and even kill civilians. Through political consciousness-raising, the BTI and PKI encouraged critical attitudes toward cultural and economic systems that benefited local rulers and landowners. The land reform campaign of the BTI and the PKI captured the sympathy of many farmers and teachers and therefore was seen as a threat to the interests of local aristocrats. Churches in NTT also viewed the increasing influence of the PKI as a threat. The Evangelical Christian Church of Timor and the Christian Church of Sumba rejected the PKI, stating that communism denies God and creates enmity amongst social-economic classes.[4]

The macro context of this tragedy was the Cold War. Several researchers have shown that the 1965 Tragedy in Indonesia was also fed by global tensions between the United States and the USSR. Bradley Simpson reveals that the Tragedy was ultimately about national and global grabs for political and economic power. The Western bloc's aid to the Indonesian Army was driven by an ulterior motive, namely to gain access to Indonesia's oil reserves, precious minerals, cash crops, and forest products.[5] U.S. aid to the Indonesian military to quell the PKI required that, in the end, Indonesia had to give U.S.-based companies power over Indonesian natural resources and had to adopt a capitalist economic system. In fact, the suppression of Communism in Indonesia effectively removed President Soekarno, who had been moving the country strongly in the direction of socialism, from power.

NURTURING SOLIDARITY: JPIT

Formed in 1999, the Eastern Indonesian Women's Network (JPIT) is a network comprising more than forty women of different faiths from regions in eastern Indonesia. Members of this network focus on publishing research related to women, religion, and culture. In March 2010, JPIT's governing board agreed that the 1965 Tragedy would be one focus of research. Because the research on 1965 cannot be separated from the need to do theology in the local NTT context, JPIT worked with the Theology Faculty of Artha Wacana Christian University (UKAW) Kupang, NTT. This partnership was motivated by the fact that a major driving force of this research came from professors and alumnae of the UKAW Theology Faculty.

Members of the research team were women ministers and candidates for ministry willing to risk doing research on a topic that for many is still taboo. Initially we, as researchers, thought this research would include offering pastoral care to grandmothers who have experienced trauma for years. However, our experience with them has taught us that the trauma related to this humanitarian tragedy touches our lives as well and that solidarity can never be a one-way process. By coming together, we give to and take from each other; we care for each other. This mutual support has enriched the lives and faith of both young and old who participate in Elderly Prayer Friends.

LEVELS OF ADVOCACY, LAYERS OF HEALING

The advocacy that began with research has evolved into a process of healing for grandmothers and researchers alike. Walking in solidarity with the survivors as they struggle for their rights gives us and other members of JPIT courage to confront and slowly recover from our own fears.

Individual Healing

We found three types of victims during the research. Some refused to speak. The depth of bitterness and despair resulting from the execution of loved ones, and fear that their stories could have a negative impact on living relatives, continues to silence these women. A second group was willing to be interviewed, but refused for their stories to be shared publicly.

These women regarded our visits and questions to them as pastoral ministry and so wanted their stories to remain in the individual space of pastoral care. A third group shared their stories enthusiastically. One informant, who was arbitrarily fired as a civil servant, told us, "I knew that God would someday send people to hear my story." These individuals wanted their stories to be heard and published, and wanted to be involved in follow-up activities, including Elderly Prayer Friends.

Prior to the launching of *Forbidden Memories*, Grandma Bessie commented: "We once lived in a hole, but JPIT has brought us out of it." Discrimination and stigma are metaphorically like a dark and musty hole. Nevertheless, friendship among the survivors and support from JPIT has enabled the women to speak in public. This has contributed to their transformation to become women with self-confidence, free of fear. Through friendship, they reclaim their dignity and nourish hope that sustains the struggle to clear their names and rehabilitate their rights. Thus, JPIT's advocacy process is simultaneously a healing process. Grandma Penlaana lives on the island of Alor. After her husband was killed, she alone raised her children in the midst of family and social discrimination. After her story was published in *Forbidden Memories*, Gandma Penlaana said, "When I die, I will smile in my coffin because now I am really happy."

Through participation in Elderly Friends Prayer and participatory advocacy, these women no longer must face stigma or painful memories alone. They know they did nothing wrong and now join other women who also struggle for social justice and to restore their good names.

Family Healing

The impact of 1965 on the wives and children of men who were killed has been severe. What they experienced, in fact, was more than just incidental impact; it was an extension of the violence established through legislated forms of discrimination supported by an elaborate bureaucratic system. Fifteen years after the height of the massacres, Indonesia's interior minister still issued an order for the surveillance and control of those accused of involvement in an attempted Communist coup. This order was followed by a presidential decree known as *litsus* (*penelitian khusus,* "special investigation"). All individuals applying for government service were subjected to "special investigation" to prevent the possible resurgence of Communist influence through government channels. The *litsus* ruling, in fact, was applied not only to those accused as members of PKI, but also to second-generation, even third-generation family members of all those detained or killed.

The New Order's[6] successful bureaucratization of discrimination by executive order demonized not only suspected Communists, but members of their families as well. As a result, families were torn apart. Beginning with the events of 1965–66, many family members distanced themselves as far as possible from their "Communist" relatives, sometimes by changing their family name. In some cases, people would even identify family members as Communists in a bid to protect themselves or to gain access to family wealth and property. Some parents did all they could to prevent their children from knowing anything about their past. Their fears are not baseless. Even today, street banners may still warn of the latent dangers of the PKI.

A comparison of two women survivors makes the point about family healing. Sarlota was a teacher in Sabu when her husband was executed in 1966. She lost her job until 1977 (when she was reinstated with a partial salary) and for years had to report to the local police. She raised three small children and now lives in Kupang to be closer to them and her grandchildren. In a body-mapping exercise in which Sarlota matched emotions to organs, it became clear her children know her story.

> Her head is a source of strength: I am still given healthy thoughts.
>
> Her heart: I do not feel revenge towards anyone; I still watch over my children so they too do not seek revenge on those who once committed evil, either towards family members or others in society.
>
> She gives thanks for her hands and feet: They still work . . .

Yohana, on the other hand, lived with trauma for many years, and poor health kept her from joining Elderly Prayer Friends. She once told Paoina, "I still lack self-confidence. What if someone should suddenly raid my house and find this book [*Forbidden Memories*]? What then?"

In 1963 Yohana became head of the Kupang branch of Gerwani, a progressive women's group mistakenly considered by many to be a wing of the PKI. In 1966, Yohana was arbitrarily arrested, was detained for several weeks, and lost her job as a teacher. Then without warning in 1975 Yohana was again arrested at her home. She was forced to leave her eleven-month-old daughter, whom she was still nursing, with her husband. She and two other friends from Gerwani were imprisoned in Bali for three years.

We experienced a contrast in the dynamics of these two women's families. When Grandma Sarlota was hospitalized with a bad back, we visited her and met members of her family who, upon learning we were from JPIT, greeted us warmly. The conversation was comfortable. A few months later Grandma Yohana died. When we attended her wake, her daughter asked how Karen knew her mother. When Karen started to explain and was met with a confused look, she quickly steered the conversation in another direction. Mery later reminded Karen that Grandma Yo had never told her children the story about 1965 that she had entrusted to JPIT.

These brief encounters suggest that Sarlota's children, well aware of the pain their mother has endured, love and deeply respect her. Sarlota hid nothing from her children and this, in turn, has enabled the family to accept their past as something survived together. Yohana's children had a different relationship with their mother. They confided that their mother had been strict and didn't listen well to them. Although she was active in her local church, Yohana died without her family knowing her fully. Severely punished for once leading a socially active women's organization, Yohana continued to suffer for much of her life and, it seems, died with bitterness in her heart without her children able to understand it. A comparison of these two stories illustrates that a key to healing family relations is openness.

Institutional/Community Healing

The 1965 anti-Communist Tragedy not only destroyed individuals and tore apart social solidarity, but it was also an attack on local cultures and religions. President Soekarno's government recognized six official religions: Islam, Protestantism, Catholicism, Hinduism, Buddhism, and Confucianism. After 1965, Suharto's New Order government, in a blatant expression of anti-Chinese sentiment, dropped Confucianism from the list. Citizens who did not belong to one of the five official religions, including followers of indigenous religions and Confucianism, were considered atheistic Communists. Because their lives were threatened, most of them quickly converted to an officially recognized religion. Because Christianity is the dominant religion in NTT, most converts chose to become members of Protestant or Catholic churches.

At the same time, a spiritual revival that began in South Central Timor spread to other areas of NTT. One characteristic of this movement was purification of faith that viewed indigenous cultural and religious practices as heresy. As a result, both state laws and a religious movement contributed to the decimation of traditional religion and culture. This included physical self-destruction when Timorese used coal-heated irons to burn off traditional tattoos on their bodies and tribal elders cut off their traditional hair buns that were believed to be the source of their wisdom. Indonesia quickly became a modern nation by adopting world religions and modern cultures while demolishing its own.

Although it may seem as if Christianity benefited from the anti-Communist movement because it triggered an explosion in church membership, the church actually suffered both institutionally and in terms of fellowship. In the face of massive state violence, the church lacked courage to protest. The church's self-censorship regarding human rights violations began in 1965 and continued during the New Order's thirty-two-year regime. Church discrimination against victims and their families included prohibition from communion or election to church councils. Some churches refused to baptize victims' children; others required them to participate in a special worship service to confess their sin before reinstatement into full fellowship with the congregation. The church discriminated against victims and their families while honoring the perpetrators with important positions in the church.

JPIT and Elderly Prayer Friends have initiated several advocacy efforts. In October 2014, some members of Elderly Prayer Friends spoke on a live radio program broadcast by the Evangelical Christian Church in Timor's radio station. Voices of victims could be heard and listeners' direct responses, which were also aired, were sympathetic. Besides that, an edition of the monthly church bulletin covered the stories of a few survivors. We hope these steps will initiate a communal healing process within the church.

National Healing

Following the fall of Suharto in 1998, significant political reforms became possible. Indonesia ratified the international Convention Against Torture, established a commission on human rights and one to oppose violence against women, passed legislation on human rights, and sought to establish a special human rights court and a truth and reconciliation commission. However, the mechanisms and political will required for these reforms to repair the impact of past violence and prevent its recurrence do not exist. Police continue to abuse detainees, perpetrators convicted of serious human rights violations in the human rights court have all been acquitted on appeal, and the law to establish the truth commission was subsequently rescinded by Indonesia's Constitutional Court.

Such impunity allows abuse and violations to continue unabated. Indonesian civil society, however, also continues to resist this reality and, in the case of the 1965 Tragedy, has expanded the space for narratives that counter official government accounts. Several publications document civil society attempts to heal the social contract between the state and its citizens that has been repeatedly ripped to shreds by state violence or the state's neglect of victims of this violence.[7]

The Year of Truth (2013–14) initiative by the Coalition for Justice and Disclosure of Truth documented incidents of violence and impunity in Indonesia from 1965 to 2005. JPIT, as a member of this Coalition, sponsored a public hearing in April 2013, at which several women from Elderly Prayer Friends shared their stories. For many of those present this was the first time they had heard narratives that contradicted the government's account of 1965. As the Coalition itself states among its ten reasons for the Year of Truth:

> The younger generation does not yet know about Indonesia's dark history of violence. Formal history lessons still do not present history based on the truth. However, a great nation . . . can learn from its bitter past and confess its mistakes with humility.[8]

National healing in Indonesia must include confession by the state for past violence and its continuing neglect of victims' rights. However, confession must lead to political reforms able to eradicate impunity that allows criminals to reign and victims to be silenced. Initiatives such as the Year of Truth contribute to healing the brokenness of Indonesia's past as a way to a brighter future.

BENEDICTION

Indonesians have been shaped by an official account of 1965 that distorts what actually happened. A supposed Communist plot to overthrow the government by a small group of Communists became the excuse for massive slaughter and years of widespread intimidation for which no one has ever been held accountable. If this reality of impunity is not overcome, then we remain vulnerable to the possibility of massive violence in the future. If we refuse to listen, really listen, to what the Elderly Prayer Friends tell us, which demands a response of appropriate words and deeds, we can never heal as individuals, as communities, or as a nation. Let us listen to these agents of healing.

QUESTIONS FOR STUDY AND DIALOGUE

1. Have you ever thought you were helping someone only to realize that you yourself were the one being helped?

2. What are some things people are afraid to talk about in your family, church, community, or nation?

3. How is past conflict dealt with in your family, church, community, or nation?

4. Who are the marginalized groups in your church or community and why are they marginalized? Do you know them personally?

5. Does your church understand advocacy as part of its ministry? If so, advocacy for whom?

6. This article discusses several circles of healing: individual, family, local community (including communities of faith), and national. What about your context?

V | DEVELOPING RESOURCES

9

MARY, MARTHA, AND MONEY

Tom Morse

MOST OF US have been taught from a young age not to talk about money: How much do you make? How much do you have? How much did it cost? They are all supposed to be off the table. Money, the surplus or shortage of it, can be a major source of tension in friendships, at the workplace, and even in marriages. So is it any surprise that when money is involved in relationships with mission partners things can get complicated?

This chapter looks at the attitudes we bring with our gifts and provides a few examples of how we can support the ministries of partners through the promotion of understanding and empathy (and look out—we *are* going to talk about money).

WHY SHOULD I GET INVOLVED?

The pessimist looks at the world and says, "Every day something new and awful happens. With my few resources there is nothing I can do to address the problems I see in my community, let alone globally. What is the point in even trying?" The optimist looks at the world and says, "The world is getting better. It's going to take a long time, but eventually things will work out without my interference." They might even let themselves off

101

the hook by using the familiar quote of Martin Luther King Jr.—"The arc of the moral universe is long, but it bends towards justice."[1]

If you are reading this book, you probably find both of those options unsatisfactory, so I'd like to introduce you to a third option—meliorism. Simply put, the world is broken but can be made better through our actions in God's mission. I think if we revisit Dr. King's quote in the context of his life, we would see that the arc of the moral universe can be bent toward justice through our actions. Global challenges can be thought of in a similar way. We could wait for the long arc to eventually correct systems and structures, but can we accept choosing to allow suffering to continue when we have the capacity to participate in addressing these issues today?

If we believe that the world can be made better, we might need to find some common understanding of "better." Does it necessarily require the accumulation of wealth and things? What makes a life "better" and who makes that determination? How should we choose the projects we support financially?

Philosopher Martha Nussbaum makes the argument that gifts can be made either towards the fulfillment of needs (charity) or toward the flourishing of human capacity (philanthropy). This school of thought asserts that needs should be guaranteed through rights and provided for by institutions (like government). These rights can be seen in the Millennium Development Goals set out by the United Nations—access to water, basic education, health care, and the like. At the other end of this spectrum, voluntary giving expands the realm of capacity—such as art museums, libraries, and swimming pools—in other words, gifts that enrich the quality of life. This philosophy would encourage individuals to advocate for greater access to basic needs while giving for a better quality of life.

The writings of St. Thomas Aquinas suggest that instead of thinking in terms of "charity" or "philanthropy," we ought to return to the original meaning of "caritas," loving-kindness. Caritas is the kind of love that God shares with humanity and, as Aquinas believed, it is the kind of love that also unites all of humanity. In this light, we give bread not out of our love of bread or out of a desire to alleviate our own discomfort in knowing that others suffer, but out of a love for others that wants them to have the bread they desire.

By giving in the spirit of caritas, the understanding of a better life is reshaped, not by what the donor believes, but by the hopes and dreams of those whom we know God loves and who are brought into relationship through our sharing.

WHEN DOES MONEY GET IN THE WAY?

Imagine that an individual, who has been quite successful in her own business, is considering making a gift to a microcredit organization in another country. The donor requests the right to decide which loans are approved. After all, the individual wants to make sure her donated funds are used wisely and feel that her own success in business will be useful in guiding the microcredit group.

Now imagine a group of women gathered in a small community who for years have been working together to help each other start businesses that generate modest income and strengthen their families. What happens to this group when an outsider decides they should compete with each other for funding? Will they look to start businesses that have meaning for themselves? Will they be tempted to propose ideas that fit the donor's ideas of success? Is a person who has practiced business in the United States going to have special insights into rural communities far away? What is the power dynamic between the donor and the beneficiary?

Every gift is a wish by the donor for the life of the recipient. Does that wish put the donor's conception of the good life on a pedestal above what the recipient may want? Recipients may not be in a position to refuse potentially life-changing gifts, even if their life changes in a way that they did not choose. This attitude in giving may come with the best intentions, but it is a mode that gets in the way of the partnerships in which Christ calls us to participate.

104 | DEVELOPING RESOURCES

A biblical example of this can be glimpsed in the home of Mary and Martha (Luke 10:38–42). Both women desired to build a deeper relationship with Jesus but went about it in different ways. Martha decided that the best way was to prepare a meal for Jesus. However, instead of helping her sister in the kitchen, Mary sat at Jesus' feet and listened. Martha complained to Jesus that her sister wasn't doing her share of the work, and Jesus took a moment to correct Martha's thinking about what is truly important.

Both Mary and Martha desired to be in relationship with Christ, but Martha did not pause to ask how she could be in relationship. Instead, she made an assumption based on her culture and context of how a relationship should begin without considering the recipient of her hospitality. Often we see individuals with the purest hearts seeking to engage with partners financially without pausing to consider whether or not there might be additional ways to participate in the relationship.

This is not an impulse that is easy to control. One Global Ministries missionary, who had been determined to serve as an equal with the partner, found himself skewing decisions at the very first meeting he attended. He sat quietly at the edge of the table listening to the community leaders' ideas over the course of the meeting, taking in each person's thoughts concerning what goals the community should set and which ministries would be their priorities. By the end of the meeting, he felt that he had successfully demonstrated his equalness with them and cautiously added his own input to the chorus of voices. As soon as he finished speaking, the discussion ended and a decision was reached that unanimously agreed with the missionary's point of view.

What he had not been aware of was that even though as pastors they were equal in one sense, his position as a white missionary from the United States gave his voice far more weight in the discussion. In addition to the issues related to colonialism and paternalism, his idea came with the implicit suggestion that funding would be attached to it. This shifted the discussion away from what might be best for the community to what could be funded for the community. Since the community did not have to fund the project, any benefit provided, no matter how small, was acceptable because the community was not investing its own funds in the project. This lack of "ownership" is often one of the root causes of failed development projects around the world.

MONEY THAT STRENGTHENS RELATIONSHIPS

"If you have come here [with your gifts] to help me, you are wasting our time. But if you have come [with your gifts] because your liberation is bound up with mine, then let us work together."

In revisiting this well-known quote from Lilla Watson, I've only recently realized that it applies equally well to the idea of saving someone with the Bible as it does to trying to save someone with our wallets. If our attitude is not one of mutuality, then we might just be "wasting our time." So how do we support the ministries of international partners in a way that recognizes our interconnectedness? How do we affirm local initiative without asserting control?

Projects Aren't Partners

We as North Americans have been taught to be skeptical of giving to projects that we can't put our hands on. After a series of scandals in the early 1990s, overhead and operational expenses were thought of as the hallmark of poorly run organizations. Instead, projects were the things that "smart" donors supported. We want to give the gifts that dig wells, build homes, and equip hospitals. Don't get me wrong—gifts through Global Ministries like these do *incredible* things and change thousands of lives each year, but, at the end of the day, it's awfully tricky to be in relationship with a well.

When I stopped to consider the ways in which I was giving, I realized that it didn't really reflect my values and beliefs. I care about individuals and communities and their hopes and dreams. I want to share in their successes and walk with them through times of trouble in the deeper sense of caritas. So why was I writing checks for things instead of people?

When thinking of the massive global challenges we are seeking to address, we have to recognize that no one person or group has the resources —economically, technologically, politically, culturally—to resolve them on their own. In order to bend the moral arc of the universe towards justice, we are going to have to work together.

Partners Aren't Projects

We also have to recognize that when we give a gift to a project, it is a partner that makes it possible. If we truly care about the partnership, we can't act as though the partner only exists to complete the projects we fund. If we really are in relationship with the partner, we have to make sure that the first step we take in gift giving is listening to their priorities. In this way, our gifts affirm their vision for their own communities and help us avoid taking a controlling role in the ministries in which we are seeking to accompany them. Otherwise, we risk thinking of our international partners as projects and damaging our relationships.

This is not to say that partners do not have a responsibility to guard the integrity of their vision. In fact, some communities in Haiti have grown so tired of groups uniformed in matching T-shirts foisting unwanted goods upon them that they have established their own committees to decide which organizations they will work with. By reasserting their agency, they have been able to set priorities for their community while engaging in committed partnerships that are focused on long-term growth rather than one-time experiences.

Partners Are Partners—Projects Are Projects

When partnerships are fully realized, we are together able to combine our strengths and minimize our weaknesses. In creating new ministries, international partners create local stakeholders who are invested in the success of the project. As a result, the project is designed in light of local ways and conditions and in the appropriate scale of what can be utilized and maintained. This leaves space for the partner to articulate a local understanding of the causes of this challenge. We can then play a number of roles in supporting this ministry, including prayer for discernment as the project is developed and prayer for its success; physical support in assisting with construction or maintenance; financial support after the project has been articulated and continued support as the ministry expands; and advocacy around the underlying issues that create the necessity for such a project. These roles allow us to join in partner ministries without jeopardizing the integrity of our partners' vision for their community.

The power of this model of working together can be seen in the medical ministries of the Community of Disciples of Christ in the Congo (CDCC). The challenge was expanding access to basic health care in rural communities. How might this be accomplished? Maybe additional clinics should be built in these communities, but it turns out there aren't enough doctors to staff them. Maybe we should arrange transportation from the villages to the hospitals in the cities, but roads are scarce in the Congo and the trip along the river is much too far for most patients to make.

The ideas that come to our minds reflect our understanding of how health care works in the United States. Without a deep knowledge of local conditions, it would be next to impossible to come up with the solution that was found by the CDCC—a hospital boat! Congolese doctors make the long journey to remote villages, and the basic supplies, generators, sterile equipment, heat sensitive medications, and vaccines that require refrigeration are transported on the boat to serve the many villages that don't have electricity. Once their vision was in place, the CDCC was able to secure the necessary support from partners. The hospital boat has been a tremendous success, treating hundreds of patients who would otherwise not have access to medical care each month.

WHAT IS THE LOCAL IMPACT OF GLOBAL GIVING?

When the Upper Midwest Region of the Christian Church (Disciples of Christ) agreed to support the appointment of Reverend Anne Gregory to be a missionary in Thailand, they had no doubt that they would be enriched by the experience. Anne was a child of missionaries who had grown up in Thailand, and now, after serving as a pastor in Iowa and becoming active in the region, she was receiving a new calling—to serve with the Church of Christ in Thailand.

A year later, they found that experience to have been overwhelmingly positive. Not only did the region succeed in supporting a missionary presence, but they helped to reengage congregations that had been seeking an outlet to express their passion for God's mission in the world.

Regional Minister Bill Spangler-Dunning says, "The experience renewed relationships between congregations and the region, and together we accomplished something much bigger than any congregation could have on its own. This renewal of regional connections allows us to dream more boldly about the future. It also served as an invitation for congregations to join an exciting movement with real global impact." Given this reaction, it is not surprising that the leadership of the region found that missional giving did not reduce the funds that were available for local and regional ministry.

Other congregations, conferences, and regions have experienced that connecting with God's global mission provides an opportunity to be reminded that we, as Christians, are called to serve beyond the four walls of the church, beyond the boundaries of our community, and beyond the borders that seek to divide us from our brothers and sisters around the world.

FUNDRAISING THAT EXPANDS UNDERSTANDING

Each year the worst charity appeals are nominated for an award known as the "Rusty Radiator." These ads use a sense of pity in the donor to elicit funds—but to move the donor to this feeling they utilize depictions that perpetuate stereotypes and damage the dignity of the economically disadvantaged. They might show a child in tattered clothes walking barefoot through muddy streets in search of food, or show a mother clutching her starving child while saying, "She is waiting for you to save her life." You might even remember the "super group," Band-Aid, in the late 1980s that sang, "There's a world outside your window; And it's a world of dread and fear; Where the only water flowing is the bitter sting of tears."[2] These efforts might be successful in raising funds for projects, but we should not underestimate or brush aside the incredible damage they do to the people they are trying to help.

In developing your own resources and campaigns to raise funds that support the ministries of international partners, there are three questions to keep in mind:

1. Does it motivate sympathy (pity) or empathy (caritas)?
2. Does it give agency to the donor or to the beneficiary?
3. Does it affirm the dignity and complexity of the people with whom we are walking?

When you keep these questions in mind, you will be creating appeals that foster a greater sense of caritas within the donors that invites them into relationship with those they want to help. You will also be countering the damaging notion that people living in difficult circumstances have no ideas of their own or motivation to move beyond their present station. In this way, your efforts will reflect the value you have placed on working in partnership.

CONCLUSION

Money has the potential to make relationships rather messy *and* the potential to help partner ministries reach their full potential. It takes a willingness to pause and listen, it takes caritas to set aside our own plans, and it takes intentionality in our giving, but the reward of this effort is the realization of the hopes and dreams of partners and communities. The outcomes are not always easily measured in gallons, pounds, or hours, but in the richness of the relationships that God calls us to be a part of.

QUESTIONS FOR STUDY AND DIALOGUE

1. Create an inventory of the issues you feel are most critical for a "good life" and rank five to ten issues that you feel are essential. Are these issues of "charity" or "human flourishing"?

2. Consider the gifts of time and treasure you made in the last year. Do they reflect the issues you feel most passionate about? What connects you to the organizations that you give to?

3. How does your congregation utilize mission dollars? Does the process take into account the voices of beneficiaries?

Fundraising ideas that restore dignity and nourish hope

- Organize a walk-a-thon carrying buckets of water to promote empathy and understanding of the chores that children around the world perform because of a lack of access to clean water.

- Share success stories from recent mission efforts and invite friends to be a part of the next effort.

- Invite refugees or immigrants to speak to your group to better understand the situation from a different point of view.

- Challenge friends to make a tithe that offsets the resources they consume, whether that is fossil fuel, conflict minerals in technology, or something else related to your cause.

How does Global Ministries give in partnership?

Global Ministries walks with partners in identifying their priorities. Once these are articulated, Global Ministries engages donors who are in relationship with the partner and encourages new donors to consider the ways in which God is calling them to participate in mission. This process helps donors to establish and maintain healthy relationships and avoid the pitfalls described in this chapter. Each year, thousands of individuals, congregations, regions, conferences, and organizations are able to provide the support that assists partners in helping their communities to experience the fullness of God's abundant life.

To learn more about current giving opportunities, visit http://www.global ministries.org/special_projects.

10

LEARNING FROM OUR GLOBAL PARTNERS

Linda McCrae

"WE OFFER OUR PRAYERS for the Community of Disciples of Christ in the Democratic Republic of the Congo, and most especially for our partners in the Mbandaka District, as word has been received of confirmed cases of the Ebola virus that have led to two deaths at this point with a number of other infected persons." So read the e-mail message sent in August 2014 by our regional minister of the Christian Church in Indiana, and suddenly what had seemed a strange and faraway health crisis became a family matter.

Wait a minute, there's Ebola in Mbandaka? These are our partners! We have been in a covenantal relationship since 2008. They have visited us. We have sent people to visit them. We have seen photos. Our Indiana campers have raised money to purchase school supplies for kids in Mbandaka. We have prayed for one another. And now they are being threatened by Ebola?

The Ebola virus in the Mbandaka District turned out to be a less dangerous strain than the deadly one in other places we had heard about from news reports, but the truth remained: We are connected to our global partners. And that is the first lesson we receive through our partnerships around the world. We are no longer separate.

This learning is a gift because it moves us closer to God's vision of humanity. After creating the world with everything in it, including humanity, God "saw everything that [God] had made, and, indeed, it was very good" (Gen. 1:31).

It also moves us closer to God's vision of the church where Christ "in his flesh . . . has made both groups into one and has broken down the dividing wall" (Eph. 2:14) and where "there is no longer Jew or Greek, there is no longer slave or free, there is no longer male and female; for all of you are one in Christ Jesus" (Gal. 3:27).

There is a song that is sung during the Jewish holiday of Passover called *Diyenu*. A rough translation of that Hebrew word is "it would have been enough." That word comes to mind as I think about our global partners. If this gift of connection were the only gift we received from them, it would have been enough. But no, there's more! Everybody would have their own list, but here are some of the things I have seen that we can learn from our global partners.

RESOURCEFULNESS

I'll never forget the day I arrived at the airstrip on an army base in a remote area of northwestern Guatemala to board the small plane that would carry me back to Guatemala City. I was traveling with a couple of Guatemalans, and we watched as the plane landed and turned off its motor while unloading the few passengers and cargo. When we had boarded for the return trip, the engine would not start.

My immediate thought was: How long does it take to get a plane mechanic to northwestern Guatemala? The pilot, meanwhile, got busy working on another solution. He tinkered with the engine, trying everything he could think of, to no avail. Finally, he pulled a thick rope out of the plane and called to four soldiers who were nearby to come and help. He wound the rope around the propeller shaft and instructed the soldiers to pull as hard as they could (imagine how you start a lawnmower). He loaded us up and climbed in the cockpit, the soldiers pulled, the engine started up, and off we went!

If we had depended on a mechanic showing up (my solution to the problem), I don't know how long we might have waited. Many of our global partners, like that pilot in Guatemala, focus on the resources they have, including what may be their most reliable resource—their God-given wits.

We learn from our global partners that what we have is often enough to solve the problem in front of us. As residents of countries where there are experts and specialists in everything, we in North America tend to look outside of ourselves for solutions. While there's certainly a role for experts and specialists, we might discover that we have more resources than we thought we did.

Diyenu . . . that would have been enough!

RESILIENCE

Nelson Mandela, the former president of South Africa, spent twenty-seven years in prison because of his opposition to the racist apartheid regime and emerged to lead South Africa into a new era. Mandela is cited as an example in many areas—leadership, forgiveness, courage, equality, and dignity, to name a few.

For me, Mandela and the whole country of South Africa teach a lesson of resilience. Along with the rest of the majority black or colored population, our partners in that country were victims of oppression and violence for many years. They organized and resisted and stood up to the unjust government. They suffered huge losses in the process. From the outside, it seemed like they would never overcome. Yet they persevered and achieved their freedom, and rather than being distorted by the wrong that was done to them, they maintained a spirit of openness, generosity, and forgiveness.

We learn from our global partners that the human spirit is strong and able to overcome adversity.

Diyenu . . . that would have been enough!

JOY

How can we learn about joy from people whose lives are so different from ours? In particular, how can we learn about joy from people whose lives are so much more difficult than our own, generally middle-class and privileged lives? Many of our global partners live in poverty, with all of its life-threatening challenges. Lack of health care and education, environmental threats, scarcity, and oppression and violence combine to make life quite precarious for many of our sisters and brothers. When I imagine myself living that kind of life, joy is the furthest thing from my mind.

And yet, when we gather with our partners, joy abounds. A few years ago, Rev. Ilumbe of the Disciples of Christ in Mbandaka visited congregations in Indiana. In spite of language challenges, he exuded joy, especially when he picked up his guitar and sang, "What a Friend We Have in Jesus," a favorite hymn in the Congo.

When I worked with Guatemalan peasants, we would often end our workshops or assemblies with an evening of *actos culturales*—"cultural acts," meaning an impromptu show put on by the participants, who would sing or recite a poem or put together a skit. Invariably the evening would include great amounts of laughter and applause as we made our own entertainment.

Anyone who has visited our partners in the Congo comes away moved by the moment of offering in the worship services, where people dance their way forward to put their small contribution in a basket up front and dance their way back to their seats, accompanied by upbeat singing and drumming. The offering time can last ten or fifteen minutes while people make two or three rounds through the church, filled with the joy of offering themselves and their resources to God. We learn from our global partners that joy has less to do with our circumstances and more to do with connecting what is inside us with other people or with God.

Diyenu . . . that would have been enough!

FAITH

Our partners in the Democratic Republic of the Congo punctuate their daily lives with prayer and song. When I arrived in Mbandaka a few years ago, before leaving the airport our partners gathered with us in a circle and sang praise to God for a safe arrival. Every day when we climbed into a van or stepped into a canoe that would take us to our destination, our hosts prayed aloud, asking for God's care and guidance for that day.

I learned another lesson of faith from Manuel, a man in Guatemala whose wife and several of his children were killed in a massacre by the army during the 1980s, a time in their country that they refer to as "the violence." He and his two sons survived. The younger of his sons, at age five, had been present and watched the massacre happen from a hiding place.

Fifteen years after Manuel's family's deaths, I stood with him near the spot where they had lost their lives. He broke down crying as he talked about the massacre, but after he composed himself, he went on to talk about the meaning of their suffering: "Before the violence, we were afraid to say anything. Now our suffering has taught us not to be afraid and to speak up."

Manuel taught me that day how suffering can be redemptive when it brings us closer to God and God's realm. The end of his story was not loss but courage. He helped me to see that while God does not choose for us to suffer, God is with us in the suffering with the power of the resurrection

We learn from our global partners to see God in new ways through our different experiences and lenses. In many cases we learn from them of a radical dependence on God. It is not our bank accounts and jobs and insurance policies that bring security to our lives, but God, who is our constant companion.

Diyenu . . . what gifts we have received through the lessons of our global partners! Resourcefulness, resilience, joy, and faith are some of the qualities I have observed through my own connections with our global partners. These experiences have transformed my way of thinking and my faith.

More transformative still has been the kind of learning that comes from the very act, over time, of being in partnership. Through engagement with others who are different from ourselves we learn greater sensitivity. We learn empathy. We learn more about ourselves.

North American Christians live in a society that emphasizes the individual and individual responsibility. While responsibility is an important characteristic, its positive aspects are sometimes outweighed by an obsessive focus on the self. We're encouraged to focus on our well being, on our family's economic situation, on our country's place of power in the world. The value of community is minimized in the worldview we absorb.

As we engage with our global partners, our worldview is expanded, especially when we can critically examine the nature of differences between us. We discover that the comfort and privileges we enjoy are due more to an accident of birth than as a result of our hard work. We better understand the way economic and political systems shape human lives. We realize at a deeper level how much we have in common with other human beings, even while the differences are significant.

A transformed worldview changes the way I live my life. When I return to the United States after having been with people who must carry all their water from a stream or a common spigot, I am extremely conscious of the amount of water I use on a daily basis. When I stand in the grocery store and contemplate the multiple options I have for every single item on my shopping list, I remember the limited choices that I've seen in other countries. These new realizations can lead to new habits: I may consume less, I may give away more, I may dedicate time to analyzing and changing the unjust structures of our world.

Clearly there are many lessons to be learned from our global partners. The next question is how we connect with them. Where do we start? And where do we go from there?

LEARNING FROM OUR GLOBAL PARTNERS | 119

The first way that many congregations engage in global partnership is by giving money. In some ways, it's the easiest kind of engagement. If our congregation participates in Our Church's Wider Mission, Disciples Mission Fund, One Great Hour of Sharing, Week of Compassion, or other denominational channels for regular or special giving, we are engaging in partnership.

Our congregation in Indianapolis has designated a portion of its capital campaign receipts in recent years to building projects with our partners in Mozambique, the Democratic Republic of Congo, and Haiti. As we prepared for each campaign, we contacted Global Ministries so that we could educate ourselves about the realities and needs of our partners around the world, and we chose a project that was a high priority for our partners.

Raising money is one important way to engage, but hopefully it will not be the only way. There is no question that congregations in North America have financial resources to share, but if our only connection is through the money we send to our partners, our relationship is a one-way street and we'll miss out on the rich gifts that our partners have to share with us.

A partnership is different in that it goes both ways. It's a two-way street. Committed relationships potentially create a new dimension in the same way that marriages are qualitatively different from friendships. As a pastor, I often say to couples that the depth of learning or growth in a marriage or committed partnership is proportionate to the depth of commitment, openness, vulnerability, and critical engagement that each of them contributes to the relationship. If we engage partners with commitment and an openness to being transformed, we learn the most profound lessons of life, like how to love, live well and faithfully, and relate to God and humanity.

One of the great challenges of global partnership is how to move from a relationship of unequal parts toward a more mutual relationship. In many situations, we in North America are the ones with the most material resources and therefore the most power to shape the relationship. How do we enter into partnerships in a deeper way, in a way that affirms the different but equally valid resources brought by each side of the partnership? How do we as North Americans lay aside our privilege and our worldview in order to enter into the world of another so that we may be transformed by the lessons we learn?

For almost thirty years, Needham Congregational Church, located outside of Boston, has had a partnership with Santa María Tzejá, a Mayan indigenous community in northwestern Guatemala. Manuel, whose story I told earlier, lives in this village. The partnership began in the mid-1980s after a period of violence in which the army had destroyed this village along with hundreds of others. Families fled with the few possessions they could carry and hid in the mountains for up to a year and a half. Eventually about half of the people returned to their village under the control of the army, while the other families went to Mexico as refugees for more than ten years.

Since 1987, the church has sent dozens of delegations to Guatemala and received several groups from Santa María Tzejá. Clark and Kay Taylor led this project for the Needham Congregational Church for many years and in the process learned valuable lessons about how to connect with partners. Clark shares these pieces of advice:

- Take all the time it takes to build trust with people. Be there with them and let them come to you. With the Guatemala Partnership of a church with a village in Guatemala, building on the experience of weeklong in-the-village delegations, it took some years to get that trust developed. We took relatively small amounts of development money each time as a good faith gesture, but they made all the decisions about how the money would be used. They also made proposals to us, some of which we could manage, but others we couldn't. Trust was built in that process.

- Go often enough to get known, then become absolutely dependable about showing up when you say you will. Another part of building trust.

LEARNING FROM OUR GLOBAL PARTNERS | 121

- Invite people to come and visit you as well. When they do, receive them with hospitality and share your culture and context while opening space for them to share as well. Reciprocal visits can be a wonderful way for your larger church and community to engage actively in relationships.

- Engage for the long haul. So many healthy bells and whistles have developed in our relationship for staying with it over some years.

- Build for mutuality. At first the people told us: You will be rewarded by God for what you have done. We don't hear that anymore as the relationship has made clear that we benefit mutually.

- You may want to select one area important to them and you in which you invest more of your resources. Like all decisions, that should come with both partners in full agreement. We selected the payment and training of teachers for the schools—primary and middle school.

The people of Needham Congregational Church have learned that trust, dependability, endurance, mutuality, and investment are crucial to building healthy and sacred relationships. We too can enter into partnership with a commitment to these values. It requires time and effort, thought and prayer, but when we build this kind of partnership, the reward is great for both our partners and us.

In 1 Corinthians 12, the apostle Paul used the wonderful image of the body of Christ to describe the church. We're not all feet or hands, or ears or eyes. We are different, but we are all important to the functioning of the body. When one member of the body suffers, all suffer together. When one member is honored, all rejoice.

Partnership offers us the opportunity to live out our call to be the body of Christ, bringing joy, transformation, and hope along the way. Thanks be to God for the gift of partnership!

122 | DEVELOPING RESOURCES

QUESTIONS FOR STUDY AND DIALOGUE

1. How are the lessons we learn through our global partnerships different from what we learn about other countries through mainstream media?

2. How have you experienced resourcefulness and resilience in your own life? Where have you seen it in others, either in your own country or in other countries?

3. How does Manuel's story of losing his family resonate (or not) with your understanding of suffering and loss? Where do you see God in situations of violence and suffering?

4. In your own spiritual growth, what part comes from or through individual activities (prayer, study, service, etc.) and what part comes from or through the communities of which you are a part? How can you expand your community to include more global partners?

notes

FOREWORD

1. Emile Brunner, *The Word and the World* (London: SCM Press, 1931), 108.

INTRODUCTION
Mission in the Twenty-first Century

1. bell hooks, *Teaching to Transgress: Education as the Practice of Freedom* (London: Routledge, 1994), 61. Terms in brackets are mine.

2. Angel Riba, Charismatic Catholics, translation by Juan Cardoza-Oquendo and Carlos Cardoza-Orlandi.

CHAPTER 1
Partnership: Pitfalls and Possibilities

1. Max Warren, *To Apply the Gospel: Selections from the Writings of Henry Venn* (Grand Rapids, MI: Eerdmans, 1971), 26–27.

2. Waldron Scott, "The Fullness of Mission," in *Witness to the Kingdom: Melbourne and Beyond,* ed. Gerald H. Anderson (Maryknoll, NY: Orbis, 1982), 50.

3. "Report of an International Consultation on Relationships in Mission: Bangalore, 19–22 May 1996" *International Review of Mission* 86 (1996), 285.

4. Valdir Raul Steuernagel, "Reflections on the Athens Conference," *International Review of Mission* 94 (2005), 433.

123

124 | NOTES

5. Brunner, *Word and the World*, 108.

6. J. Andrew Kirk, *What Is Mission? Theological Explorations* (London: Darton, Longman & Todd, 2002), 184.

7. Aelred Stubbs, ed., *Steve Biko: I Write What I Like* (Johannesburg, South Africa: Heinemann Press, 1978), 68.

8. D. Preman Niles, *From East to West—Rethinking Christian Mission* (St. Louis: Chalice Press, 2004), 44.

CHAPTER 3
Receiving in Partnership: Opening Our Hearts

1. Pope Francis, "Letter to a Non-Believer: Pope Francis responds to Dr. Eugenio Scalfari, journalist of the Italian newspaper *La Repubblica*," 4 September 2013, © Copyright Libreria Editrice Vaticana, https://w2 .vatican.va/content/francesco/en/letters/2013/documents/papa-francesco _20130911_eugenio-scalfari.html.

CHAPTER 5
Mission and Interreligious Dialogue: The Case of Christians and Muslims in the Middle East

1. Pew Research Center, "Latest Trends in Religious Restrictions and Hostilities," February 26, 2015, http://www.pewforum.org/2015/02/26 /religious-hostilities/.

2. *Majmu`at al-watha'iq as-siyasiyya l-il-ahd an-nabawi w'al-khalafa ar-rashida"* compiled by Muhammad Hamidullah, 6th ed. (Beirut, Lebanon: Dar an-Nafa'is, 1987). Translation from the Arabic is mine. See also John Andrew Morrow, ed., *The Covenants of the Prophet Muhammad with the Christians of the World* (Kettering, OH: Angelico Press/Sophia Perennis, 2013), 109–138.

3. Ibid.; Morrow, *Covenants of the Prophet*, 65–98.

4. "Dialogue and Coexistence: An Arab Muslim-Christian Covenant," document resulting from the December 18–20, 2001, session of the Arab Group for Muslim-Christian Dialogue, Cairo, Egypt, article 2, http://www.agmcd.org/files/pdfcovenant.htm.

NOTES | 125

5. "Dialogue and Coexistence," articles 22, 24.

6. The Institute for Ecumenical and Cultural Research (IECR), *Living Faithfully in the United States Today* (Collegeville, MN: IECR, 2001).

CHAPTER 6
Evangelism: Reconciling with God, Reconciling with Others

1. "Action Plans of the Reformed Church in Hungary's Service Among Roma," 13th Synod Cycle, 12th session, http://www.reformatus.hu/data /documents/2014/01/30/Action_Plans_of_the_Roma_Strategy_of_the _RCH_finalized_1.pdf.

2. Reformed Church in Hungary website, "Our Call," http://www .reformatus.hu/mutat/6820/.

3. *Together towards Life: Mission and Evangelism in Changing Landscapes,* ed. Jooseop Keum (Geneva, Switzerland: WCC, 2013), article 79.

4. Letty M. Russel, *Just Hospitality: God's Welcome in a World of Difference* (Louisville: Westminster John Knox, 2009), 21.

5. The Evangelical Pentecostal Union of Venezuela (UEPV) is a national organization of Pentecostal churches that emerged in Venezuela in 1957. It is linked historically and theologically to the first Pentecostal movement that became known in the country, founded by Pastor Frederick Bender Geother in Barquisimeto, Lara State, in 1922.

6. Neo-Pentecostal churches are considered by some scholars to be a new version of Pentecostalism.

7. The Valencia Letter is an official document of the UEPV, approved on its XXXI Convention held in the Christian Community *"El Triunfo,"* Valencia, on August 29, 1987. The document expressed a public statement about the UEPV intentions to claim their Pentecostal identity, but with an ecumenical option as well as commitment to mutual cooperation with Pentecostal, Evangelical, Protestant or other confessions. For more information, see Carmelo Álvarez, *Compartiendo la Misión de Dios: Discípulos y Pentecostales en Venezuela* (Quito, Ecuador: Ediciones CLAI, 2007), 41–42.

CHAPTER 7

Changed through Serving: Engaging in Advocacy

1. U.S. Border Patrol, "Border Patrol Strategic Plan: 1994 and Beyond," 6, http://cw.routledge.com/textbooks/9780415996945/gov-docs/1994.pdf.

2. Paulo Freire, *Pedagogy of the Oppressed* (New York: Continuum Books, 2007).

CHAPTER 8

How Can Advocacy Heal?

1. Mery Kolimon and Liliya Wetangterah, eds., *Memori-Memori Terlarang: Perempuan Korban & Penyintas Tragedi '65 di Nusa Tenggara Timur* (Kupang: Yayasan Bonet Pinggupir, 2012). This book documents and analyzes memories of women survivors of the 1965 Tragedy in the eastern Indonesian province of East Nusa Tenggara (NTT). Most women in Elderly Prayer Friends first knew each other as participants in this participatory research that JPIT conducted from 2010 to 2012. An English translation of this book was published by Monash University in 2015 with the title *Forbidden Memories: Women's Experiences of 1965 in Eastern Indonesia.*

2. Kolimon and Wetangterah, *Memori-Memori Terlarang,* 377.

3. John Roosa, *Dalih Pembunuhan Massal: Gerakan 30 September dan Kudeta Suharto* (Jakarta: Indonesian Institute of Social History and Hasta Mitra, 2008), 250–53. This is the Indonesian translation of Roosa's book that was first published in English as *Pretext for Mass Murder: The 30th September Movement and Suharto's Coup d'État in Indonesia* (Madison, WI: University of Wisconsin Press, 2006).

4. Kolimon and Wetangterah, *Memori-Memori Terlarang,* 350–51.

5. Bradley Simpson, "The United States and the International Dimension of the Killings in Indonesia" in *1965: Indonesia and the World,* ed. Bernd Schaefer and Baskara T. Wardaya (Jakarta: Goethe-Institut Indonesien Gramedia Pustaka Utama, 2013), 43–60.

6. "New Order" was a term coined by Suharto when he came to power in 1966 to distinguish his pro-capitalist government from former President Soekarno's increasingly socialist government. The term is now commonly used to refer to the period of Suharto's dictatorship from 1966 to 1998.

7. Examples of such publications include: *Taking a Stand: Four Decades of Violence against Women in the Journey of the Indonesian Nation* (National Commission to Oppose Violence Against Women, 2009); *Derailed: Transitional Justice in Indonesia Since the Fall of Soeharto* (a joint report by the International Center for Transitional Justice and the Commission for the Disappeared and Victims of Violence, 2011); and *Menemukan Kembali Indonesia: Memahami Empat Puluh Tahun Kekerasan demi Memutus Rantai Impunitas* [*Rediscover Indonesia: Understanding Forty Years of Violence to Break the Chains of Impunity*] (Year of Truth Report of the Coalition for Justice and Disclosure of Truth, 2014).

8. *Menemukan Kembali Indonesia*, 13.

CHAPTER 9
Mary, Martha, and Money

1. King used the phrase many times, recasting the words of nineteenth-century abolitionist and Unitarian minister Theodore Park (1810–60).

2. Band-Aid, "Do They Know It's Christmas?" 1984 charity single with music/production by Midge Ure, lyrics by Bob Geldof, Warner/Chappell Music, Inc.

recommended reading

CHAPTER 1
Partnership: Pitfalls and Possibilities

Barnes, Jonathan. *Power and Partnership: A History of the Protestant Mission Movement*. Eugene, OR: Pickwick, 2013.

Cardoza-Olandi, Carlos. *Mission: An Essential Guide*. Nashville: Abingdon, 2002.

Niles, D. Preman. *From East and West: Rethinking Christian Mission*. St. Louis: Chalice, 2004.

CHAPTER 2
Mission in a Globalized World

Bosch, David J. *Transforming Mission: Paradigm Shifts in Theology of Mission*. American Society of Missiology Series, No. 16. Maryknoll, NY: Orbis Books, 2008.

Kalu, Ogbu U., Peter Vethanayagamony, and Edmund Kee-Fook Chia, eds. *Mission after Christendom, Emergent Themes in Contemporary Mission*. Louisville: Westminster John Knox, 2010.

Matthey, Jacques, ed. *You Are the Light of the World: Statements on Mission by the World Council of Churches 1980–2005*. Geneva: WCC, 2005.

Walls, Andrew, and Cathy Ross. *Mission in the 21st Century: Exploring the Five Marks of Global Mission*. Maryknoll, NY: Orbis Books, 2008.

129

CHAPTER 3
Receiving in Partnership: Opening Our Hearts

Corbett, Steve, and Brian Fikkert. *When Helping Hurts: How to Alleviate Poverty without Hurting the Poor . . . and Yourself.* Chicago: Moody, 2014.

Elmer, Duane. *Cross-Cultural Servanthood: Serving the World in Christlike Humility.* Downers Grove, IL: Intervarsity, 2006.

Lederleitner, Mary T., and Duane Elmer. *Cross-Cultural Partnerships: Navigating the Complexities of Money and Mission,.* Downers Grove, IL: Intervarsity, 2010.

Lingenfelter, Sherwood, and Marvin Mayers. *Ministering Cross-Culturally: An Incarnational Model for Interpersonal Relationships.* Ada, MI: Baker Academic, 2003.

Lupton, Robert D. *Toxic Charity: How Churches and Charities Hurt Those They Help, and How to Reverse It.* New York: HarperCollins, 2011.

Shoemaker, Shirley, and Herb Shoemaker, eds. *Team Training Manual for Sister-Church Partnerships.* Lehigh Acres, FL: Reciprocal Ministries International, 2011.

CHAPTER 4
Relationships: Why and How We Serve

Crabb, Larry. *Connecting: Healing Ourselves and Our Relationships.* Nashville: Thomas Nelson, 2005.

Okun, Barbara, Jane Fried, and Marcia L. Okun. *Understanding Diversity: A Learning-as-Practice Primer.* Belmont, CA: Wadsworth, 2010.

Zoli, Andrew, and Anne Marie Healy. *Resilience: Why Things Bounce Back.* New York: Simon and Schuster, 2012.

CHAPTER 5
Mission and Interreligious Dialogue: . . . the Middle East

Matlins, Stuart, and J. Magida. *How to Be a Perfect Stranger: The Essential Religious Etiquette Handbook.* Woodstock, VT: SkyLight Paths, 2015.

Matlins, Stuart, and J. Magida. *How to Be a Perfect Stranger: A Guide to Etiquette in Other People's Religious Ceremonies, Vol. 2.* Woodstock, VT: Jewish Lights, 1997.

Niebuhr, Gustav. *Beyond Tolerance: Searching for Interfaith Understanding in America.* New York: Penguin, 2008.

Speight, R. Martin. *God Is One: The Way of Islam.* New York: Friendship Press, 2001.

CHAPTER 6
Evangelism: Reconciling . . .

Hungary

Gonda, László. *The Service of Evangelism, the Evangelism of Service: The Impact of John R. Mott, Hendrik Kraemer, Johannes C. Hoekendijk, Willem A. Visser 't Hooft on the Development of the Understanding of Mission in the Reformed Church in Hungary, 1910–1968.* Zoetermeer: Boekencentrum, 2008.

Kool, Anne-Marie. *God Moves in a Mysterious Way: The Hungarian Protestant Foreign Mission Movement (1756–1951).* Zoetermeer: Boekencentrum, 1993.

Kool, Anne-Marie. "A Protestant Perspective on Mission in Eastern and Central Europe." *Religion in Eastern Europe,* XX/6, 1–21.

Kool, Anne-Marie. "Trends and Challenges in Mission and Missiology in 'Post-Communist' Europe." *Mission Studies* 25 (2008)/1, 21–36.

Korea

Christian Conference of Asia and International Christian Network for Democracy in Korea, ed. *Reunification, Peace, and Justice in Korea: Christian Response in 1980s.* Hong Kong: CCA Publication, 1988.

Cumings, Bruce. *Korea's Place in the Sun: A Modern History.* New York, London: W. W. Norton, 2005.

Paik, Nak-Chung. *The Division System in Crisis: Essays on Contemporary Korea.* Oakland, CA: Global, Area, and International Archive, University of California Press, 2011.

Weingartner, Erich. "Twentieth Anniversary Reminiscences on the Tozanso Process: Ecumenical Peace Efforts in Korea." In *Windows into Ecumenism: Essays in Honor of Ahn Jae Woong*, 374–80. Hong Kong: CCA, 2005.

Venezuela

Álvarez, Carmelo. *Compartiendo la Misión de Dios: Discípulos y Pentecostales en Venezuela*. Quito, Ecuador: CLAI, 2007.

Piedra, Arturo. *Evangelización Protestante en América Latina: Análisis de las Razones que Justificaron y Promovieron la Expansión Protestante*. Quito, Ecuador: CLAI, 2002.

CHAPTER 7
Changed through Serving: Engaging in Advocacy

Ho, Christine G.T., and James Loucky. *Humane Migration: Establishing Legitimacy and Rights for Displaced People*. West Hartford, CT: Kumarian Press, 2012.

Miller, Todd. *Border Patrol Nation: Dispatches from the Front Lines of Homeland Security*. San Francisco: City Lights Books, 2013.

Paley, Dawn. *Drug War Capitalism*. Oakland, CA: AK Press, 2014.

Regan, Margaret. *Detained and Deported: Stories of Immigrant Families under Fire*. Boston: Beacon, 2015.

CHAPTER 8
How Can Advocacy Heal?

Fackenthal, Jeremy D. "The Problem of Coming to Terms with the Past: A Post-Holocaust Theology of Remembrance." Claremont Graduate University Theses & Dissertations. Paper 33, 2012, http://scholarship .claremont.edu/cgi/viewcontent.cgi?article=1033&context=cgu_etd.

ICTJ and Kontras. "Derailed: Transitional Justice in Indonesia Since the Fall of Soeharto," 2011 joint report, https://www.ictj.org/sites/de-

fault/files/ICTJ-Kontras-Indonesia-Derailed-Report-2011-English
_0.pdf.

Philpott, Daniel. "What Religion Brings to the Politics of Transitional
Justice," *Journal of International Affairs* 61(1): 93–110, http://papers
.ssrn.com/sol3/papers.cfm?abstract_id=1417035.

Rambo, Shelly, "Resurrecting Scars," *Feminism and Religion*. Online blog,
April 9, 2012, http://feminismandreligion.com/2012/04/09/resurrect
ing-scars-by-shelly-rambo/.

Rambo, Shelly, *Spirit and Trauma: A Theology of Remaining*. Louisville:
Westminster John Knox, 2010.

Thaler, Kai. "Foreshadowing Future Slaughter: From the Indonesian
Killings of 1965–1966 to the 1974–1999 Genocide in East Timor,"
Genocide Studies and Prevention: An International Journal 7/2 (2012):
204–22, http://scholarcommons.usf.edu/cgi/viewcontent.cgi?article=
1038&context=gsp.

Movies and Videos

Oppenheimer, Joshua. *The Act of Killing*, 2012. Oppenheimer focuses on
one perpetrator of the 1965 killings in the area of North Sumatra and
invites him to reflect upon and reenact his acts of killing. Movie reviews
available online; for example, https://www.themonthly.com.au/issue
/2013/october/1380549600/luke-davies/joshua-oppenheimer-s-act-
killing.

Oppenheimer, Joshua. *The Look of Silence*, 2014. A son from a family of
1965 survivors confronts neighbors who were among 1965 perpetrators.
He and his family struggle to live in a country where the truth of the
1965 crimes is silenced. Movie reviews available online; for example,
http://www.theguardian.com/film/2015/jun/07/joshua-oppenheimer-
the-look-of-silence-interview-indonesia.

Udall, Tom (Dec. 10, 2014). Senator Tom Udall (New Mexico) Introduces
Resolution on Reconciliation in Indonesia, http://govne.ws/item/Tom-
Introduces-Resolution-on-Reconciliation-in-Indonesia#.

CHAPTER 9
Mary, Martha, and Money

Banerjee, Abhijit, and Esther Duflo. *Poor Ecomomics: A Radical Rethinking of the Way to Fight Global Poverty.* (Philadelphia: Public Affairs, 2011)—This book explores different types of development projects around the world and asks the question "Did they make a difference?" A great read for those wanting to understand the difficult decisions faced by the materially poor.

Illingworth, Patricia, and Thomas Pogge. *Giving Well: The Ethics of Philanthropy* (New York: Oxford University Press, 2011)—A more academic approach to the ethical complexities of giving. It poses more questions than answers but will definitely challenge the way you relate to the world around you.

Rustyradiator.com—to see the best and worst charity appeals each year. There is also great original content that Global Ministries has used in youth and adult curriculums.

Sider, Ronald. *Rich Christians in an Age of Hunger: Moving from Affluence to Generosity* (Nashville: Thomas Nelson, 2005)—Provides a biblical framework of justice in relation to global challenges and argues that Christians around the world possess the resources for addressing these challenges but have chosen not to.

CHAPTER 10
Learning from Our Global Partners

Be a Global Mission Church! http://www.globalministries.org/global_mission_church.

Child and Elder Sponsorships, http://www.globalministries.org/child_sponsorship.

Church to Church Partnerships, http://www.globalministries.org/church_to_church_partnerships.

Missionary Relationships, http://www.globalministries.org/missionary_relationships.

RECOMMENDED READING | 135

People to People Pilgrimages, http://www.globalministries.org/people_to
_people_pilgrimages.

Renewing, Engaging, and Advocating Churches (REACH), http://www
.uccfiles.com/reach/.

Revolutionary, Engaged, and Driven Youth (READY), http://uccfiles.com
/ready/.

contributors

CO-EDITORS

JONATHAN BARNES, PhD, serves with the Mennonite Central Committee as country representative to South Africa, Lesotho, and Swaziland. He previously served Global Ministries for thirteen years, ten as a mission personnel in South Africa and Mozambique and three as executive of Mission Education based in Indianapolis. He holds a PhD in Theology and Development from the University of KwaZulu-Natal in South Africa (2010) and is the author of *Power and Partnership: A History of the Protestant Mission Movement* (Eugene, OR: Pickwick, 2013).

PETER E. MAKARI, PhD, has served as executive for the Middle East and Europe with Global Ministries of the United Church of Christ and the Christian Church (Disciples of Christ) since July 2000. For two terms, he also served ecumenically as the co-chair of the National Council of Churches' Interfaith Relations Commission (2008–13). He earned an MA in Middle East Studies from the American University in Cairo (1993) and a PhD in Politics and Middle East Studies from New York University (2003). He is the author of *Conflict and Cooperation: Christian-Muslim Relations in Contemporary Egypt* (Syracuse, NY: Syracuse University Press, 2007).

137

CHAPTER AUTHORS AND EDITORS

JONATHAN BARNES, PhD, serves with the Mennonite Central Committee as country representative to South Africa, Lesotho, and Swaziland. He previously served Global Ministries for thirteen years, ten as a mission personnel in South Africa and Mozambique and three as executive of Mission Education based in Indianapolis. He holds a PhD in Theology and Development from the University of KwaZulu-Natal in South Africa (2010) and is the author of *Power and Partnership: A History of the Protestant Mission Movement* (Eugene, OR: Pickwick, 2013).

GRACE BUNKER comes from a long line of Congregational UCC missionaries. She grew up in Sri Lanka and South India, attending Kodaikanal School. After graduating from Earlham College, Grace taught elementary school in several U.S. states and in Dubai, United Arab Emirates, and Mexico. From 2001 to 2005 she was a Global Ministries missionary in Jaffna, Sri Lanka. She now is retired and happily active in Casas Adobes Congregational UCC in Tucson, Arizona.

PHYLLIS M. BYRD has served in Kenya for twenty-six years. She started her ministry working at the All Africa Conference of Churches during the leadership of Rev. Jose Chipenda and Archbishop Desmond Tutu. Phyllis at present works with the Organization of African Instituted Churches as the director of the Just Communities program. Phyllis is also one of the associate ministers at St. Andrew's Presbyterian Church. She hails from New York City and is a member of Hollis Avenue UCC. Phyllis is married to Polycarp Omolo Ochilo, a professor at the University of Nairobi. They are blessed with six children.

KAREN CAMPBELL-NELSON, PhD, teaches a variety of subjects, including Theology and Human Rights as well as Qualitative Research Methods at the Artha Wacana Christian University in Kupang, West Timor, Indonesia. She teaches in both formal and informal settings, and her particular skills in action research and social analysis have been developed to support the fulfillment and projection of human rights, especially of women who have endured armed and political conflict.

CARLOS F. CARDOZA-ORLANDI, PhD, is professor of World Christianities and Mission Studies at Perkins School of Theology, Southern Methodist University. He co-authored with Justo Gonzalez *To All Nations from All Nations: A History of the Christian Missionary Movement,* which received the 2013 Book Award for Excellence in Missiology by the American Society of Missiology. He was a member of the Common Global Ministries Board (UCC and CCDC) and the Division of Overseas Ministries (CCDC) Board. He is an ordained minister of the Iglesia Cristiana (Discípulos de Cristo) en Puerto Rico and the Christian Church (Disciples of Christ) in the United States and Canada. He is actively involved in cross-cultural mission and interreligious encounters and dialogues in local communities and with partners in Latin America and the Caribbean.

JUDY CHAN, PhD, serves as executive secretary for Communications at the Hong Kong Christian Council. She is a member of National Capital Presbytery in Washington, D.C.

PRINCE DIBEELA, PhD, is the former general secretary of the United Congregational Church of Southern Africa. He has previously been principal of the Kgolagano Theological College and has served the world church in several positions, including being moderator of the Council for World Mission and member of the Central Committee of the World Council of Churches.

DEREK DUNCAN is associate for Global Advocacy and Education and NGO representative to the United Nations for Global Ministries of the Christian Church (Disciples of Christ) and United Church of Christ. His work focuses on policy advocacy and congregational education related to peace, human rights, and other challenges facing international partners and communities. He studied religion and politics with a focus on Muslim-Christian relations at Harvard Divinity School, where he earned an MDiv, and American Religious History at Vanderbilt University.

ELENA HUEGEL, an educator, storyteller and writer, serves with Global Ministries at the Shalom Center, a peace building, environmental education and spiritual development camp in the Andes Mountains of Chile. She is the daughter and granddaughter of Disciples missionaries and has a Master's Degree in Conflict Transformation and Peace Education.

MERY KOLIMON, PhD, completed her studies at the Protestant Theological University in the Netherlands in 2008. She is currently teaching Missiology and Contextual Theology at Artha Wacana Christian University in Kupang, West Timor, Indonesia. She is also the director of the Postgraduate Program of the University and the coordinator of the Eastern Indonesia Women Network for Study on Women, Religion, and Culture.

LINDA MCCRAE has served since 2002 as pastor of Central Christian Church in downtown Indianapolis, Indiana, where she gets great joy from being part of an inquisitive, diverse, justice-seeking community of faith. Her previous experience in ministry includes six years as a missionary in Mexico and Guatemala, and five years as pastor of Wood Memorial Christian Church in Van Buren, Arkansas.

SUSAN MCNEELY is retired from Eli Lilly and Company after working as a pharmaceutical chemist and packaging consultant for twenty-five years. She is a member of the Congo Partnership Committee of the Indiana Region of the Christian Church (Disciples of Christ). In 2014, as part of the partnership with the Mbandaka Post of the Disciples of Christ in Congo, she spent three months teaching English to church leaders and living with Congolese friends.

JEFFREY MENSENDIEK was born in Buffalo, New York. Since the age of three when his parents were assigned as UCC missionaries, Sendai, Japan, has been his home. Jeffrey has a BA from Bucknell University, an MA from the Pacific School of Religion, and an MDiv from Eden Theological

Seminary. He now lives in Kobe, Japan, where he works as chaplain at Kwansei Gakuin University.

BEVERLY EILEEN MITCHELL, PhD, is professor of Historical Theology at Wesley Theological Seminary, in Washington, D.C., where she teaches courses in theology, church history, and human rights. Dr. Mitchell has contributed to several World Council of Churches (WCC) ecumenical resource documents published on the WCC's website.

TOM MORSE served as a Global Ministries–appointed missionary in China for five years before beginning his work in the office of Resource Development. He has a passion for helping individuals and congregations connect their values and vision with the exciting work of international partners in ways that affirm the dignity and dreams of both. Tom currently serves as the executive for Mission Education and Interpretation in the Indianapolis office of Global Ministries and is working toward a master's degree in Philanthropic Studies.

CATHERINE NICHOLS, PhD, earned her MA in Women's Studies and her PhD in Social Welfare from Brandeis University. She has served as the executive for Mission Personnel for Global Ministries and as vice-president of the Christian Church (Disciples of Christ) Division of Overseas Ministries since 2012. Catherine previously served as mission personnel in Jerusalem, with the Sabeel Ecumenical Liberation Theology Center, from 2001 to 2009. She also served on the Division of Overseas Ministries Board of Directors from 1988 to 1996.

SCOTT NICHOLSON is a long-term volunteer missionary with Global Ministries who is blessed to serve with the Home of Hope and Peace (HEPAC) community center in Nogales, Sonora, Mexico.

MAJAHA NHLIZIYO, an ordained minister serving in the United Congregational Church of Southern Africa (UCCSA) has served the church and communities of southern Africa in various ministerial and leadership ca-

142 | CONTRIBUTORS

pacities for the past twenty-eight years. Serving with missionary mentors and colleague ministers Allen Myrick as well as Sandra and Daniel Gourdet has been a great demonstration of partnership in mission.

BALÁZS ÓDOR is a pastor in the Reformed Church in Hungary. He currently serves at the Synod Office and, since 2009, leads the Ecumenical and International Department. He formerly taught Systematic Theology at the Theological Seminary in Pápa (2001–12). He also led the Youth Department in the Synod Office (2003–08) and was a university chaplain (2001–02).

ELIDA QUEVEDO is a bishop and ordained pastor of the Evangelical Pentecostal Union of Venezuela. She serves ministerially in the area of theological education, liturgy, and women.

MOHAMMAD SAMMAK is a founding member of the Arab Group for Muslim-Christian Dialogue and serves on its Executive Committee. He is also the secretary general of the Christian-Muslim Committee for Dialogue in Lebanon, and a member of the Islamic Spiritual Summit in Lebanon. He serves on several boards—including the King Abdullah Ben Abdel Aziz Center for Interreligious and Intercultural Dialogue (Vienna, Austria) and the Al al-Bayt Organization (Amman, Jordan)—and on the World Council of Religions for Peace (New York). He is the author of twenty-eight books.

SHIN SEUNG-MIN currently serves as the director of the Just Peace, Reunification, and Ecumenical Forum of the National Council of Churches in Korea (NCCK). He formerly served as the ecumenical officer of the Presbyterian Church in the Republic of Korea (PROK), regional secretary of the World Student Christian Federation Asia-Pacific Region, and executive secretary of the Human Rights Desk for the NCCK.

CONTRIBUTORS | 143

PETER SHOBER has served for the past twenty-five years as senior pastor, University Congregational UCC in Missoula, Montana. A past president of the Montana Association of Churches, he has a passion for ecumenical justice work and exploring the intersection of wilderness and spiritual practice.

GLORIA VICENTE CANÚ is a K'iche'/Kaqchikel Maya born in Guatemala and raised in the United States. Her family migrated to the United States as a result of the thirty-six-year-old civil war that took place in Guatemala. More than thirty members of her father's family were victims of the war. Raised most of her life in Chicago, she studied International Studies at DePaul University. She is married to Santos Domingo Par Vasquez, a K'iche' Maya, and they are parents to three children. She has been serving in Guatemala since 2007.

BRUCE VAN VOORHIS is a Global Ministries missionary who has served several regional organizations in Hong Kong for twenty-five years—Documentation for Action Groups in Asia (DAGA), the Asian Human Rights Commission (AHRC), and currently the Asia and Pacific Alliance of YMCAs (APAY), where he is assigned as a coordinator of the regional youth network Interfaith Cooperation Forum (ICF), a joint program of APAY and the Christian Conference of Asia (CCA) in Chiang Mai, Thailand. He holds a Bachelor of Journalism degree from the University of Missouri and a Master's degree In International Relations from Boston University.